Your Turn!

STORIES OF RENEWAL

Dear Marjorie,

For all the drafts you read
along the way, your encouragement
and support, and the privilege
of living on this dirt &
gravel road that Rooster
finds — my deepest gratitude.

with love,

Elle

Your Turn!

STORIES OF RENEWAL

Edited by Carol S. Lawson & Robert F. Lawson

CHRYSALIS BOOKS / *Swedenborg Foundation Publishers*

THE CHRYSALIS READER is a book series that examines themes related to the universal quest for wisdom. Inspired by the concepts of Emanuel Swedenborg, each volume presents original short stories, essays, poetry, and art exploring the spiritual dimensions of a chosen theme. Works are selected by the series editors. For information on future themes or submission of original writings, contact Editor Carol S. Lawson, 1745 Gravel Hill Road, Dillwyn, Virginia 23936.

©2008 by the Swedenborg Foundation Publishers

LIBRARY OF CONGRESS CATALOGING-IN-PUBLICATION DATA
Your turn!: stories of renewal /
edited by Carol S. Lawson and Robert F. Lawson.
    p. cm. — (Chrysalis reader; v. 15)
ISBN 978-0-87785-239-1
1. Spiritual life—Christianity—Literary collections. 2. Regeneration (Theology—Literary collections. I. Lawson, Carol S. II. Lawson, Robert F., 1948– III. Title. IV. Series.

PS509.S62Y68 2008
810.8'0382—dc22

CHRYSALIS BOOKS
Swedenborg Foundation Publishers
320 North Church Street
West Chester, Pennsylvania 19380

FRANKLIN HAY

Contents

Taking the Waters

"WHAT GOES AROUND, COMES AROUND," my former college room-mate Micky says with a smile. Sitting at the potter's wheel, he molds and shapes elemental earth into cups, bowls, and plates for a wedding present. Despite a 24-7 world, where much of what happens seems out of our hands, we can choose to step aside, as Micky, a social therapist, regularly does to refresh the spirit at his potter's wheel. Likewise, the essays, poetry, and art of *Your Turn! Stories of Renewal* explore the possibilities and realities of personal transformation.

In the late eighteenth century, the curative properties of mineral water springs drew to them an increasing stream of the curious. Americans began "taking the waters" at health spas, such as Warm Springs, Virginia; Yellow Springs, Pennsylvania; and Saratoga Springs, New York. The medicinal waters varied in trace minerals and other properties, from sulfur to iron to carbonated water. George Washington hoped to cure his rheumatism at Warm Springs. Wounded Continental soldiers rested at the nation's first military hospital at Yellow Springs, hoping the water there would speed their rehabilitation. In 1771 Iroquois Indians carried their ailing friend Sir William Johnson, Superintendent of Indian Affairs, to High Rock Spring (Saratoga Springs) to help restore his health.

By the 1820s, Saratoga Springs became the health spa mecca of the north. (*Spa* is the acronym from the Roman *sanitas per aquas,* meaning *health through water.*) Known in its opulent heyday as the Queen of Spas, one could become fully immersed in the elixir of naturally carbonated water. Some doctors built sanatoriums, believing the Saratoga water could cure almost anything from chronic heart trouble and nervous conditions to temporary aches and pains. However, most chose to stay at the elegant hotels and tipple the foul-tasting water, taking several glasses before breakfast, more before lunch, and a final round before retiring at night. It is said that civilization follows art, but in this case, fashion, horse racing, and gam-

Opposite:
Dipper Boy at High Rock Spring, Saratoga Springs, New York. During the Victorian era, young boys were stationed at the various mineral springs in Saratoga to serve water to the visitors. In this view, the lad holds a long pole that he used to lower empty glasses into the cone where the spring water bubbled up. Visitors often provided a tip for the effort. Original photograph (ca. 1875) from the private collection of Robert Joki, author of *Saratoga Lost* (Black Dome Press, 1998).

bling followed the water cure. Although some came for the restorative properties of the mineral water, many came for the social interaction. One dismayed 1826 visitor wrote, "Out of hundreds in this village, but few are disposed to pass an hour in divine service. The pleasure parties and balls every evening in this village engross the attention of the old and young, sick and well, and I fear this village place will prepare more souls for destruction than those efficacious waters will ever heal infirm bodies." So much for life at the font of the Fountain of Youth!

At a deeper, spiritual level, how do people go about the business of testing the water, retooling and re-purposing their lives? This is the focus of *Your Turn! Stories of Renewal*. What if, for example, as one author conjectures, you won a complete makeover on the Oprah Winfrey Show? How long would you maintain the new hairstyle, new clothes, the new look? Perhaps you would discover that such re-inventing of one's image stops short of reaching the inner you.

Another author imagines an early summer morning, dew on the grass, a fresh breeze, and the sun slanting shadows across your path. Add to this serene moment a beautiful stranger, who surprises you by momentarily engaging you in conversation, then moves on ahead. Would you have the courage to follow, to trust your intuition?

What exactly does it take to rise like the rainbow from the foot of the storm or the phoenix bird from yesterday's ashes? In one historical piece of fiction, Tom Thumb asks this question after the burning of Chambersburg. So too does an inmate at a woman's correctional facility as she struggles to remain true to herself, despite a savage environment. Another author believes it takes the act of spirit to find renewal in a world of unrelenting change and motion.

Before healing can commence from within, a writer describes coming to the edge of human endurance and understanding and then leaping, trusting, no, *believing,* that a net will appear somewhere below. Another writer addresses head on what appears to be an insurmountable problem in a neighborhood, putting into play a community action plan, winning over one convert at a time.

In the final analysis, perhaps it is falling into or discovering one's chosen vocation, plunging into an active life with one's gifts, which brings out our best. Whether a journalist's unlikely beginning as a mediocre graduate research assistant or a housekeeping assistant's surprising interaction with a room guest, these authors capture transformative moments that come when least expected.

Your Turn! Stories of Renewal reminds us that nothing is wasted, that divine love and wisdom are never ending, that when we feel as free agents in the stream of divine providence, it is then that we are experiencing full force the "green fuse" of regeneration. And it is then that we can say without hesitation, "Look out. Coming through!"

THOMAS R. SMITH

Foot of the Rainbow

In the west the sky lifted the edge of her shawl,
and spring earth flashed green in the sunlight.
I drove south through rain, looked out
my streaming windshield at illuminated
farms framed as though in a painting.

At a crossroads I turned east: a rainbow
curved so high I had to hunch forward
over the wheel to glimpse its full arch
against the dark. Then out in a field I saw
its foot misting along a line of near

trees like a rainbow's ghost. It was that close,
moving with me, the arc I'd thought far as
mountains! So we carry our rainbows inside
us, nearer than we know, near as that moment
I followed rainbow-footed back to my town.

THOMAS R. SMITH is a poet and teacher living in River Falls, Wisconsin. His poems have appeared in hundreds of periodicals in the U.S. and abroad. His most recent poetry collections are *Waking before Dawn* (Red Dragonfly Press) and *Kinnickinnic* (Parallel Press). He teaches at the Loft Literary Center in Minneapolis. Poetry has been his spiritual practice for thirty years.

The following story opens up our collection
of original accounts of renewal
as told by forty-eight contemporary authors.
The drama of the creation week is described for us
by a scholar who is devoting many years
of her life to a prodigious task: Lisa is translating
some forty-five hundred pages of a verse-by-verse
interpretation of the first two books of the Bible.
The study was originally published in the years 1749
to 1756 in Latin as *Arcana Coelestia*, or *Secrets
of Heaven*, by Emanuel Swedenborg (1688–1772).
Lisa's efforts are part of a larger project
being undertaken by a team of translators:
the first new translation in a hundred years
of all eighteen theological works Swedenborg
saw through the press in his lifetime—
the New Century Edition
of the Works of Emanuel Swedenborg.

A Disclosure of

SECRETS OF HEAVEN

Contained in
SACRED SCRIPTURE
or
THE WORD OF THE LORD
Here First Those in
Genesis
*Together with Amazing Things Seen
in the World of Spirits & in the Heaven of Angels*

EMANUEL SWEDENBORG

Volume 1

Translated from the Latin by Lisa Hyatt Cooper
With a Reader's Guide by William Ross Woofenden and Jonathan S. Rose
An Introduction by Wouter J. Hanegraaff
And Notes by Reuben P. Bell, Lisa Hyatt Cooper, George F. Dole, Robert H. Kirven,
James F. Lawrence, Grant H. Odhner, John L. Odhner, Jonathan S. Rose,
Stuart Shotwell, Richard Smoley, and Lee S. Woofenden

SWEDENBORG FOUNDATION
West Chester, Pennsylvania

The Creation Story

THIS CHRYSALIS READER is published in honor of an eighteenth-century civil engineer and mystic, Emanuel Swedenborg, who explored the world of spirit with the eye of a scientist. The first and largest work he published after awakening to the realm of the spirit is *Secrets of Heaven*, an explanation of the inner meaning of Genesis and Exodus. From the time of this awakening, Swedenborg interpreted the Bible as portraying in vivid and concrete images the formation and development of the human psyche—the story of one's inner life, from birth to death and beyond.

The drama of the creation week not only opens this story, but encapsulates it in its entirety. Everything that the rest of the Bible tells us about the workings of our minds and hearts appears in a condensed version in the account of the seven days during which God created the physical universe. Each day represents a different stage of intellectual and emotional growth, beginning with the vague, disorganized turbulence of unconsciousness and ending in the peace and orderly beauty of oneness with God. And like a week of physical time, the stages of inner development repeat continuously, each week of growth starting where the last ended.

In what follows I interweave the Genesis text and my summary of Swedenborg's interpretation of that text, phrase by phrase.

The ornament above, depicting a spouting heart, appears on the title page of the first edition of Swedenborg's most popular work, *Heaven and Hell* (London 1758). It is not known whether Swedenborg engraved the ornament himself, but it is certainly possible because he had learned engraving from a tradesman when he was a young adult and had produced numerous engravings of inventions. The New Century Edition of Swedenborg's works, of which Lisa is one of the translators, has adopted the ornament as an emblem on each of its book covers and title pages.

The First Day

In the beginning,

Before we are reborn,

God created heaven and earth.

*we have an inner self
and an outer self,*

And the earth was void
and emptiness;

*but there is nothing good
or true in us;*

and there was darkness
on the face of the abyss.

*our flaws and misconceptions
naturally blind us.*

And the Spirit of God was
constantly moving on the face
of the water.

*God in his mercy is always
providing us with a hidden store
of true thoughts
and positive feelings.*

And God said, "Let there be
light," and there was light.

*The trigger for change is
a dawning awareness that
our goodness is not good and
that we need help from above.*

And God saw the light, that it
was good.

*The awareness comes
from God himself.*

And God made a distinction
between light and darkness,
and God called the light day,
and the darkness he called night.

*We can now see the difference
between what comes
from God and
what comes from ourselves.*

And there was evening and there
was morning,

*We move one step away from
ignorance, as God comes
into our lives*

the first day.

and we enter a new state.

The Second Day

And God said, "Let there be
an expanse in the middle
of the waters,

God now shows us

and let it exist to make
a distinction

that we have an inner being,

among the waters,
in the waters."

*but at first we do not realize
it is separate from our outer self.*

And God made the expanse,

Eventually we do see

and he made a distinction

and recognize the difference

between the waters that were
under the expanse

*between the worldly facts
that our outer self learns first*

and the waters that were over
the expanse;

*and the higher concepts that our
inner self learns afterward.*

and so it was done. And God
called the expanse heaven.

*As we become aware of our inner
self, we move toward heaven.*

And there was evening,
and there was morning,

*We take another step
away from ignorance, as God
comes into our lives*

the second day.

in a new way.

The Third Day

And God said, "Let the waters
under heaven be gathered
into one place

*What we learned at the previous
stage is registered in our memory
alongside all the worldly facts*

and let dry land appear,"

in our outer self.

and so it was done. And God
called the dry land earth,

Our outer self

and the gathering of waters he
called seas,

*and the body of knowledge
stored there*

and God saw that it was good.

are gifts from God.

And God said, "Let the earth
cause the sprouting on the earth
of the tender plant,

*We start to do
a tentative kind of good and
speak a tentative kind of truth,*

of the plant bearing its seed,

*then a more useful kind
that reseeds itself,*

of the fruit tree making the fruit
that holds its seed,

*and finally a kind that reproduces
abundantly,*

each in the way of its kind,"

*though the goodness and truth
are not yet fully alive, since they
result from self-compulsion.*

and so it was done. And the
earth produced the tender plant,
the plant bearing its seed
in the way of its kind, and the
tree making the fruit that held
its seed in the way of its kind,
and God saw that it was good.

*Everything good and true
comes from God.*

And there was evening
and there was morning,

*We move further away
from ignorance*

the third day.

*as God comes anew
into our lives.*

The Fourth Day

And God said, "Let there
be lights in the expanse
of the heavens

*Love and faith develop
in our inner being*

to make a distinction between
day and night;

*and show us the difference
between good and evil.*

and they will act as signals

*They provide clues
to our inner state.*

and will be used for seasons
for both the days and the years.

*Love and faith mature
and develop in unending cycles.*

And they will act as lights
in the expanse of the heavens
to shed light on the earth";

*They give guidance from within
to our outer self.*

and so it was done. And God
made the two great lights:

The guiding principles are

the greater light to rule by day

love,

and the smaller light to rule
by night;

a faith that reflects love,

and the stars.

*and bits of knowledge
radiating from faith.*

And God placed them
in the expanse of the heavens,
to shed light on the earth,

*Love and faith in our inner self
exert an influence
on our outer self*

and to rule during the day

*at the times when we respond
willingly to their influence*

and during the night,

and to make a distinction
between light

and darkness;

and God saw that it was good.

And there was evening
and there was morning,

the fourth day.

*and at the times when we
must compel ourselves,*

*when heart and mind cooperate
with each other*

and when they clash.

*God alone warms our hearts with
love and enlightens
our minds with faith.*

*We move from trial and anguish
to faith and kindness,*

which is a new state.

The Fifth Day

And God said, "Let the waters
cause the creeping animal

—a living soul—

to creep out.

And let the bird flit over
the land, over the face
of the expanse of the heavens."

And God created the big
sea creatures,

and every living, creeping soul
that the waters caused to creep
out, in all their kinds,

and every bird on the wing,
of every kind.

And God saw that it was good.

And God blessed them,

saying, "Reproduce and multiply
and fill the water in the seas,
and the birds will multiply
on the land."

The facts we know

come alive for the first time

in a kind of physical body.

*Our rational mind
also comes alive.*

*The new faith that we developed
at the previous stage animates
whole categories of knowledge,*

and individual facts,

*and the very way we understand
and use that knowledge.*

*It is God alone who enlivens
these intellectual gifts.*

Good things happen inside us.

*Everything with life from God
in it proliferates abundantly,
whether it is an expression
of love or faith.*

And there was evening
and there was morning,

*Emerging from the dark, we speak
with conviction, which strength-
ens the truth and goodness in us,*

the fifth day.

in a new state.

The Sixth Day

And God said, "Let the earth
produce each living soul

*We now start to act with
conviction and therefore with love*

according to its kind:

on many different levels:

the beast,

soul,

and that which moves,

mind,

and the wild animal of the earth,

and body.

each according to its kind";
and so it was done. And God
made each wild animal of the
earth according to its kind,

*Rebirth starts with our most
superficial emotions—
our cravings and appetites—*

and each beast according to its
kind, and every animal creeping
on the ground according
to its kind;

and moves deeper.

and God saw that it was good.

*It is God alone who
regenerates us.*

And God said, "Let us make
a human

*Through the agency of angels
and spirits, God endows us
with his own qualities,*

in our image,

making us spiritual,

after our likeness;

*causing us to resemble himself
and his angels.*

and these will rule over the fish
of the sea

*We now know how to make good
use of the facts we know*

and over the bird in the heavens,

and of the thoughts we think,

and over the beast,

*and of the intentions
we cherish—*

and over all the earth,

our entire being,

and over every creeping animal
that creeps on the earth."

And God created the human
in his image;

in God's image he created them;

male and female he created
them.

And God blessed them,

and God said to them,
"Reproduce and multiply,

and fill the earth

and harness it, and rule

over the fish of the sea

and over the bird in the heavens

and over every living animal
creeping on the earth."

And God said, "Here, now, I am
giving you every seed-bearing
plant on the face of all the earth

and every tree that has fruit;

the tree that produces seed
will serve you for food.

And every wild animal
of the earth and every bird
in the heavens and every animal
creeping on the earth,

in which there is a living soul—

every green plant will serve
them for nourishment."

down to the lowest levels.

*We are born again
with a new mind*

and a new heart,

which now work in tandem.

*Wonderful things happen
inside us.*

*The marriage of mind and heart
in us results in positive feelings
and true thoughts,*

which proliferate abundantly,

*despite the conflict we inevitably
face as spiritual people*

*in regard to the cold, hard facts
we know*

*and the uninspired thoughts
we think*

and the base emotions we feel.

*We receive insights that point
in a useful direction,*

and we do good in the world.

*Both the insights we receive
and the good we do nurture us.*

*Thoughts and feelings, words
and deeds, on the lowest level
of our mind, where we struggle,*

have life from God in them.

*We are sustained on this lowest
level, even if the sustenance
is minimal.*

And so it was done. And God saw all that he had done and, yes, it was very good.

And there was evening and there was morning,

the sixth day.

But because there is now a marriage of faith and love, of mind and heart, God is truly working in us.

As we emerge from the dark, love takes the lead,

which is a new experience.

The Seventh Day

And the heavens and the earth were completed, and their whole army. And on the seventh day God completed the work that he had done; and he rested on the seventh day from all the work that he had done. And God blessed the seventh day and consecrated it, because on it he rested from all the work that he had done as God in creating it.

Having been changed from lifeless people to spiritual people, we are now changed from spiritual people, who are motivated by truth, to heavenly people, who are motivated by love. The heavenly person is the seventh day, on which God rests, and is not just an image of God but a full, true likeness.

~

Swedenborg goes on to explain Genesis 2 as a depiction of a person who has become the seventh day, so to speak. Such people are vibrantly alive, perceptive, and wise, and what makes them so is love. After the struggle and vacillation of the first six days, they have arrived at their Sabbath rest. They acknowledge that it was God alone who fought their battles ("God completed his work"), and they find themselves beyond the reach of inner conflict ("and rested on the seventh day")—or at least on one level, or in one area of their lives.

One of the beauties of Swedenborg is that he never promises the static tedium of eternal sameness. When we "arrive," it is only to discover new opportunities for growth and development. After enjoying a day of rest, we wake to the dawn of our soul's new week, and the cycle begins anew.

LISA HYATT COOPER is the translator of *Secrets of Heaven* for the Swedenborg Foundation's New Century Edition of Swedenborg's works and cannot imagine a more rewarding occupation. She lives in Bryn Athyn, Pennsylvania.

I. Second Chances

BILL ELLISON

Another Day

How I love the sizzle
   of sweet country fiddleheads
      and brookies fried with these ferns,

salaciously curling
   and uncurling as they sputter,
      sprawling like similes in butter.

One whiff of these
   (O alluring infamia!)
      and I'm yanked like a nail

from the boards of sleep . . .
   or beckoned, like lust half-snoring,
      even from my churchly white outhouse

toward breakfast—
   as lurid as rust in ripe
      river raspberries,

I'm pried like a spike from the cross.

A single dad, BILL ELLISON is a painter, making his living painting seascapes and landscapes, with an occasional portrait and still life.

I Made Oprah Scream

I WAS ON THE OPRAH WINFREY SHOW, and I made her scream in front of a live audience. Can you believe that? She actually covered her mouth, bent over, came back up and let out an *ohmyGOSH!*—or words to that effect—in one sweeping, dramatic motion. All because of me. I can't remember her exact words, because I was blinded by the lights, and my legs were wobbling on those four-inch stiletto heels strapped to my ankles. So I was focused on trying not to fall and getting this whole thing over with as fast as possible.

But when I emerged from behind the curtain, there she was, waiting for me on center stage, all lit up with her Oprah smile, looking expectant (or was it impatience I saw), and then seeing her face change—the brown eyes growing big, the mouth forming a perfect O and then out came that unintelligible yowl telling me she was pleased, that I was doing okay, and that today's show was going to be a success. Imagine that. Me—a forty-three-year-old divorcee and kindergarten teacher with two kids of my own—who has nothing profound to share with the world, much less with Oprah Winfrey and her 10 million viewers. I've never written a book, never developed a tried-and-true diet, never discovered the meaning of life. I'm lucky to make it to school on time—much less understand the meaning of my own life or why I tend to be tardy. I made Oprah gasp in disbelief in front of millions. I still can't believe it happened, but it did.

MY BEST FRIEND, JULIE, who is a life coach, surprised me on my birthday. She managed to get two tickets to the Oprah Winfrey show, and she even drove us 362 miles to see it.

We live in Lake Grove, Minnesota, which is considered a bedroom community south of the Twin Cities. At one time, it was all farmland filled with miles of corn and wheat and barley that waved and *whistled* in the wind—bleeding into the hot summer sky, like some edgeless, endless amber ocean. But then developers came to town, took over the land, and parceled it out into condominiums, apartments, commercial centers, one-family homes. They rolled out miles of concrete roads, connecting everything together and stomping down any possibility of green life ever springing up again from our rich black soil.

I grew up on one of those farms—on land less than a mile away from the town home I bought after my divorce. I can't say my divorce from Mick made me a better person or uplifted my soul in any way, but it was the right thing to do. Mick is a good guy, but he wasn't ready to settle down. Still isn't, for that matter. But he makes me laugh, and, believe it or not, he's still one of my best friends. Most important, he's a good dad to our kids. Danny is ten; Gena, thirteen. Danny adores his Dad; Gena now realizes she's more of an adult than he is.

And then there was Larry. "He's tall, athletic, funny . . . *rich!*" Julie laughed when she said that. "Nice. Polite. Successful. He's perfect for you."

So Larry and I went out a few times, and as that old song goes—*zing went the strings of my heart.* How does one control the zinging tendencies of that tenderest of all organs? How do you control sensations that send you soaring to the clouds one minute, then tumbling back down to earth the next, then up again? I sure don't know.

It was the age-old struggle—head versus heart, fairy tale versus common sense. My heart told me I couldn't live without him. He turned me on. I felt alive when I was with him—excited, fulfilled. I couldn't stop thinking about him. Okay, it's corny; it's cliché, but I'll go ahead and say it anyway: *he completed me.* Okay?

But my head was telling me something else. *Whoa,* it whispered in my ear. *Step back. Take it easy; something's not right. Something's missing here. Something important. Don't rush into anything you'll regret.*

So that's what I was enduring for a month or so. My head, getting dizzy from the roller coaster ride, trying to tell me something. My heart, wanting more, not listening, luxuriating in the rush of it all. Fortunately, however, Larry made the decision for me.

"You're a wonderful woman," he said one night as we sat parked in his Porsche. "You're intelligent, funny, warm, kind, full of life. But . . ."

Well, you know the rest. He wanted to be friends, and he meant it. He really enjoyed my company and wanted me to be part of his life. And—I have to admit, he was very kind when he said this: *there is no attraction.* "I wish there were," he said, looking sincerely sad. "There isn't. But I respect you so much."

Ah, yes, respect.

I have to admit something else. I haven't been completely honest here. So this is where I'll give you the full picture, or as much as I can. Larry is CEO of a financial consulting firm in downtown Minneapolis. He owns a ten thousand-square-foot home in Lake Grove's tonier section. He wears customized silk suits, gets facials, massages, and manicures every week, and is often pictured in *Twin Cities Magazine* attending the latest fund-raiser—holding a drink in one hand and a beautiful blonde in the other.

I, on the other hand, wear the same T-shirts and jeans I've had since I was twenty-one. When it's cold, I cover them up with an old flannel shirt that's quite faded and frayed. I do that because I find them familiar and comforting. Besides, I don't have time to fuss or to figure out what I should wear today. It simplifies my life.

Now you can understand why Larry and I were not a good match—at least on a surface level, so to speak.

When dressing up, I usually wear a black skirt and white blouse; or a white blouse and black slacks. I don't fuss too much with my hair either. It's now a mousy brown streaked with gray (okay, it's gray streaked with mousy brown), and it's down to my waist. I haven't had the time (or inclination) to get it cut. On special occasions, I twist it into a bun; or I wear it in a pony tail when I'm running late (which, as I mentioned, is most of the time).

I don't have the time or patience for makeup either (or sleep, for that matter) so my eyes are a bit baggy and red-rimmed. My eyebrows have invaded my forehead—much like urban sprawl has invaded poor Lake Grove. And my skin—my best feature, actually—is starting to blotch in odd places, which I'm told is part of the aging process.

I am tall (five-foot-eleven), broad-shouldered, small-busted and have sturdy, child-bearing hips, but I have kept my small waist and thin frame.

People, being kind, have called me *handsome.* "You're a hand-some-looking woman," they'll say, or "striking" or "I bet you were once a beauty."

Well, that brings me to why I was on the Oprah show and how I made her scream. As I mentioned, Julie wanted to celebrate my forty-third birthday—and also to console me for getting dumped by Larry. Unbeknownst to me, however, the theme of this show was "surprise makeovers for deserving teachers."

Julie had nominated me for a makeover, citing my commitment to teaching, the extracurricular programs I introduced to help troubled students, my being nominated for teacher of the year, my commendations from parents, principals, and coworkers—and, of course, my T-shirts, jeans, flannel shirt, unruly eyebrows, and long gray hair. Apparently Oprah's producers felt up for the challenge.

So I was called up from the audience and tried to acknowledge everyone's applause with a gracious smile, hoping the camera didn't pick up the malevolent look I gave to Julie (who knows how much I hate such attention). Then I was hurried offstage and handed over to an army of beauty specialists, who—I swear—stepped back, frowned, and took a deep breath when they saw me coming.

Three hours later they brought me to a mirror to see my transformation. A camera crew was there to capture the moment. Needless

Cristóbal Balenciaga.
Evening Dress.
Silk, 1960–1962.
Evening Jacket.
Silk, cotton,
and sequins, 1959.
Cincinnati Art Museum.
Gift in memory
of Irma Mendelson
Lazarus. Photograph
by Walsh, 1999.

to say, I was dumfounded. Actually, there are no words to describe what I saw. This beautiful woman was standing before me. She had blond hair, highlighted in the right places and cut into a style called an angular bob. It was parted on the left, which meant I had to pull back hair that fell (like a curtain) over my right eye—a very sexy effect, Rudolfo, the stylist, assured me.

My complexion, now pink and ivory, was blemish-free, wrinkle-free, free of pores and texture and anything else resembling human skin. Gone were the pouches and puffiness I had learned to live with (where did they go? I missed them already). My eyes, dark and seductive in a way that scared me, were framed by no-nonsense brows plucked thin and pointing upwards. My fingers and toes still tingled from the buffing, poking, and polishing their nails recently endured.

The stylists decided I needed some glamour, so they chose a black cocktail dress, cut low, held up with spaghetti straps, and slit thigh-high along the side. Diamonds hung like chandeliers from my ears and in cascades around my neck. A security guard suddenly appeared to watch my every move. The shoes, they explained, called attention to my long legs, *which people would die for,* they gushed. Then they pushed me toward the curtain to get ready for the *big reveal.*

Afterwards, Oprah sent me home with the dress, the shoes, the underwear and suitcases filled with cosmetics that would last a year: foundations, concealers, blushes, brushes, lipsticks, lip liners, glosses, blemish removers, eye shadows, base shades, contour colors, mascara, eyeliners, and other "aids to maintain the illusion." She also presented me with a $5,000 gift certificate to Macy's. The security guard took custody of the diamonds and then disappeared in a cloud of dust.

Needless to say, this experience changed my life. When I got home, I was featured in several local newspapers and interviewed on Twin Cities radio and TV talk shows. At school, Bert Lomax, our principal, convened a special assembly to honor my work and present me with a plaque that will be hung "in perpetuity," he announced, in the school cafeteria.

But my students turned shy around me—which saddened me. They began to focus on the thick blond hair falling into my right eye and not on my words encouraging them to blossom and learn. Fellow teachers would compliment me on each new outfit I wore in *happy* voices that sounded forced and flat.

Gena and Danny were not as awestruck or impressed, however, which was a good thing, because it yanked me back to reality. I was merely a mom, after all.

"Let's go," Gena would yell, pounding on the bathroom door. "We're late. You've been in there an hour."

"I'm almost done. And it's only been thirty-five minutes. I've just got mascara to do, and I'll be all set."

"That's what you always say."

"Mo-o-o-m!" Now it's Danny whining at me. "I've got to pee. Hurry up."

So this gives you a sense of what went on every morning at our house, as I tried to resume a normal life, while maintaining the "look" that stunned Oprah and captured the world's admiration. But it wasn't all bad. This is also the look that brought Larry back into my life and helped me see my beautiful self in another new way.

He called soon after the show aired and, in a voice that had developed a strange purr I hadn't heard before, invited me to a cocktail party at the University Club on Summit Avenue. It was a fund-raiser for the Children's Theater, and a lot of politicians and corporate honchos would be there.

"Wear that black dress?" he murmured.

"Sure," I said. "And the same shoes?"

"Absolutely."

He didn't take his eyes off me the whole night. Nor did he remove the hand that clung to my waist and pushed me around the room, as he introduced me to friends and associates, all puffed-up and proud, like a car collector driving around a red Lamborghini and honking for attention: *See? My car's bigger than your car.*

That's when my head finally took control and talked some sense into my wishy-washy heart.

The next day I dumped a year's worth of cosmetics into a black garbage bag, tied it up with a plastic yellow ribbon and drove it to the local woman's shelter, who will distribute it to women learning to live better lives. The black dress, shoes, and silk underwear went into the garbage.

I'm keeping the new outfits I bought at Macy's, though, because they're well made and will probably last me another fifty years.

As for my sexy blond hair, I'm letting it grow out; and when it does, I'll cut it off; go short for awhile. Each morning I check the gray roots that are taking hold on the top of my head, and I feel stronger somehow, more myself. It's like watching weeds wiggle their way up through cracks in a sidewalk and slowly, inevitably, reestablishing their rightful place in a concrete world.

For twenty-five years, KATHLEEN LINDSTROM "sold her soul" to corporate America as an award-winning writer in communications and public-relations departments. Four years ago, she decided to delve into the world of creative fiction. Since then she has won the Arthur Edelstein Prize for Short Fiction. Her stories have appeared in eleven literary magazines; and her poem "Shrapnel" won first place in the 2007 Talking Stick competition.

Betty's Grandmother's Hats

Nested in the fat, round
proprietary boxes of lost shops,
a lifetime of hats curl back to front.
Betty opens them to us,
and a chorus of velvet and feathers,
brim up, brim down,
the severe, the opulent,
the black and the floral,
are borne, blinking, into daylight
on the hands of Betty's friends:
schoolteachers, ex-hippies,
military wives,
the fashionable and the oblivious,
seventeen people having tea with Betty,
and all around the table
finding something that fits.
"Why did your grandmother have
so many hats?" we want to know.
"These," Betty says,
"are only some of them."

Born in Ohio and raised in Syosset, New York, ROBIN SHECTMAN has lived most of her life in the Pasadena area. Her poetry has appeared in more than a hundred anthologies and magazines, including *American Scholar, Beloit Poetry Journal, Blue Unicorn, Borderlands, Diner, English Journal, Hawaii Pacific Review, Iris, Kenyon Review, New England Review, Poetry, Seneca Review, Sycamore,* and *Yankee.* Shectman was editor of *The Altadena Review* from 1979 to 1989. She has a chapbook, *The Century Plant,* and three un-published book-length poetry collections.

An Answered Prayer

A FILMMAKER SINCE HE WAS OLD ENOUGH TO HOLD A CAMERA, my son, Bill, and a college pal were shooting urban scenes in Portland, Oregon, when they departed from script (never a good idea). Bill slipped down an alley to relieve himself. While facing a brick wall, a police cruiser drove by and caught him in the act.

Bill told me he thought the citation was like a traffic ticket. Several phone calls later, I determined that it was more serious. Bill would have to make a court appearance. Although a defendant-friendly mechanism enabled first-time minor offenders' charges to be expunged from the record, if not handled properly Bill's knuckle-head stunt might start a rap sheet. My sister, a judge back East, advised us to hire an attorney. A federal prosecutor I knew from when our daughters played softball together agreed with my sister's assessment and recommended some defense attorneys in Portland but warned that they might run several hundred dollars per hour. That was the last thing we needed. Some summer spending and unexpected dental work already had us in the hole financially.

A couple of days before our court date, our pricey attorney discovered that, regardless of the "disorderly conduct" charge on the citation, Bill was up on indecent exposure. Explaining away disorderly conduct to future employers as a college kid prank was one thing; indecent exposure carried all sorts of terrible implications.

During the two-hour drive to Portland for Bill's court appearance, we pulled into a rest stop where a woman in a filthy sweatshirt was searching the edge of the sidewalk as if looking for change. "I thought you might be hungry," I said, handing her the untouched leftover from the bag of breakfast sandwiches I was about to trash. I swaggered back to the car feeling pretty darn saintly about how I had reached out to a stranger with a sandwich.

Once in Portland I ducked into a small public men's room near the parking garage. "Sir, can you help me please?" a crippled voice called over a stall with a wheelchair wedged in the door. The voice came from a fellow who was paralyzed down his left side and suffered a speech impediment. He was stuck in the stall. With a little jockeying of his wheelchair, we soon had him on his way.

After helping the woman with the breakfast sandwich and the half-paralyzed man, I felt good about myself. Then I saw a woman standing in front of the library selling *Street Papers. Street Papers* are a few pages of newsprint with features on issues important to marginalized citizens. People who sell the papers are often plugged into agencies that are helping them get back on their feet. Worry lines framed the woman's intelligent eyes. I sensed a story there—a factory closure, a costly family illness, outmoded skills for today's job market. When she saw me pull out my wallet, her grin added to my self-congratulatory mood. As I walked away with my paper, I waved back when she called after me, "God bless you."

At court that afternoon, our attorney moved with the aplomb of a symphony conductor. He skillfully managed to get Bill's charges reduced to disorderly conduct. After sixteen hours of community service, it would be as if the unfortunate incident had never happened. The drive home felt like two hours atop a magic carpet of relief with the renewal that a second chance brings.

An e-mail from the attorney was waiting for us when we arrived home. He told us that he was not charging us for his services as a "professional courtesy." I assumed that the courtesy was the result of our mutual association with the softball dad prosecutor. Filled with gratitude, I said to my wife, Louise, "Bread upon the waters. Those three people we helped? God rewarded us."

Despite my self-aggrandizement, I didn't feel at peace. After some reflection, a new possibility occurred to me. The woman selling *Street Papers* had called out to me, "God bless you." Perhaps because we so often hear that phrase, we forget that it is, in fact, a prayer. Whoever says it is praying for God to smile upon us. Heeding her prayer, God blessed us through the court proceedings and moved our lawyer to generosity. I'm convinced also that God intended to remind me that kindness, like virtue, is its own reward, not some *quid pro quo* with a higher power. Yes, I could feel good about my good deeds, but God didn't owe me anything back for helping people. Through the prayer of the woman selling papers, I received a gift greater than any small favor: a renewed understanding of God's power and patience.

My son was not the only one who felt humbled that day.

W.E. REINKA's essays, reviews, and articles appear in publications nationwide.

Visiting My Friend

She sees me hesitate to pet
her horse.

        The horse necks her head
further out of her stall. My friend says,
Put your forehead up against hers,
and I lean forward closing my eyes.

We stand there in silence,
the horse and I, bending to reach
each other, the rough brown hairs
between her eyes scratching the pale,
winter-patina of my brow.

I can smell horse as intimately
as I could my friend years ago.

Outside, the Equinox shifts
its silent hands in the air,

but we continue, *tête-à-tête,*
until we both seem to know
when to separate, to shuffle
away toward straw and small talk.

Now, your horse knows more about me
than you do . . .

My friend shrugs

looking away as we walk
out of the barn into the same
old repetition of Spring.

TIM MAYO holds an ALB in French language and culture from Harvard University and an MFA in writing and literature from Bennington College. His poems have appeared in *Atlanta Review* (receiving two International Merit Awards), *Babel Fruit, Del Sol Review, The Equinox, Five AM, Four Corners, Mannequin Envy, Paris/Atlantic, Poet Lore, The Rose & Thorn.* He was a semi-finalist in the "Discovery"/*The Nation* 2000 Poetry Contest. His "Dreaming of Dependable Force" was a finalist/runner-up in the 2007 *Main Street Rag* Poetry Contest, and Pudding House Publications has just published his chapbook *The Loneliness of Dogs.*

MELANIE S. BAFFES

Thin Places

Saint Martin's Cross, near Iona's Benedictine Abbey, is a "high cross" dating from the eighth century. The circle or ring is typical of Celtic crosses and represents eternity and creation. The intricate carvings are of biblical characters and animals. Photograph by Melanie Baffes, 2006.

And in that moment, the luminous One appeared
and she lifted the veil that lay over his mind.
—THE SECRET BOOK OF JOHN

THE ISLAND OF IONA IS KNOWN AS THE PLACE where Christianity first came to Scotland in 563 CE, when Saint Columba and his followers arrived from Ireland and converted Scotland and much of northern

England to Christianity. Integrating the deeply-rooted Celtic spirituality with Roman Christianity, they established a monastery on Iona, which was later destroyed by Viking invasions. In 1203, a Benedictine abbey was established on the same site, and today it is one of the best-preserved ecclesiastical buildings on the Western Isles of Scotland surviving from the Middle Ages. For centuries, this sacred island was a place of learning, Christian mission, pilgrimage, and the burial ground for several kings from Scotland, Ireland, and Norway.

The idea of pilgrimage was an important part of Celtic lore; it was a journey to seek God, to leave one's familiar home to find new life. For the Celts, the immanence of God—the presence of God in everything—was evident in the beauty and wildness of the created world. The presence of God also was found in the soul of every human being. To the Celtic imagination, not only were humans created in God's image, they were imbued with God's wisdom, passion, and creativity. Pilgrimage was more than an outward voyage to a holy site; it was an inward journey to the sacred center within.

For most pilgrims, it is the threads of Celtic spirituality that draw them to places like Iona. They are eager to circle the standing crosses, to stand at the edge of the world where land meets sea and sky, and to experience firsthand the power and mystery of this ancient tradition.

ON MY OWN PILGRIMAGE TO THIS SACRED PLACE, I walk about the abbey, the village, and the nunnery. I feel the magic of the island, so different from the places most of us inhabit. The land seems flat—at least right here—and the sky wide and welcoming. I'm reminded that as a child, I wondered why everyone focused so much on the surface of the Earth. Even then, I knew there were worlds beyond our understanding, yet we seemed to live in just two dimensions, oblivious to the vast depths and soaring heights of sea and sky. And now here, I experience another unimagined life, people living and working on a 1,800-acre island jutting boldly into the Atlantic on the western coast of Scotland. There are no skyscrapers, highways, eighteen-wheelers, bridges, or trains—this is a place rumored to have more sheep than people. I wander about the small village of Baile Mór: a few shops, a single hotel and restaurant, several dozen modest and colorful houses. What must it be like to live like this? It's as if I've entered another time.

What was Iona like when the Celts inhabited the island so many years ago? I think about what happened when Christianity came to their world. By integrating their own pagan beliefs with the new Christian way of thinking, the Celts were able to forge a faith that was true to their own origins and to the new Roman tradition as well. If you were a Celtic Christian, you believed women and men were born not with original sin but with original grace. To the Celts, the light of God was found not only in Christ, but also in each human soul; Christ came to remind us that we are made in God's image, that we carry the light and presence of God within us. I wonder if coming here now is a way to remember and awaken the collective memory of God's light and presence within each of us.

Awakening is, in fact, the theme for our group's time here on Iona. Our trip leader reminds us that, at the heart of any pilgrimage, there is always a central question. For me, the question is: *How can I awaken to a deeper life? How can I live my life as passionately, fully, authentically as possible?* I've come here to find what makes me feel most alive, although I can't say why I think I might find it on a small island in the Hebrides.

The pilgrim's path leads through the ruined nunnery, so our group gathers here for an opening prayer. While it is home to beautiful gardens, the abandoned nunnery has no roof, and it seems fitting that we worship in the open air of this glorious day. It's noisy and tourists are milling about and gawking, but we quiet ourselves to begin our day of pilgrimage.

At the only crossroads in Iona, we begin in earnest, thinking about the crossroads in our lives. Another brief prayer, and we make our way toward Columba's Bay, the ultimate destination. This is the place Columba landed when he came from Ireland, and our agreement is to walk there in silence. At last there is quiet: all we can hear now is the rustle of the wind, the occasional bleating of sheep, our boots on the path, and the sound of our own breathing.

We walk though beautiful fields with sheep and cows, and the landscape becomes hilly and rocky. This is where the crofters live, still farming and working the land, and I imagine their impatience with us tourists and hikers traipsing earnestly across their pastures. What must they think of our striving for something that comes naturally to them? The connection to the earth, to the spirit of God in the natural world—it's what we seek, but try as we might, we're strangers in a strange land.

Fresh in my mind this bright morning is *The Secret Book of John,* one of the gospels found in the Nag Hammadi desert that did not become part of the New Testament as we know it. In this secret gospel, Christ appears to John in a dream and tells him that humans have forgotten who they are, forgotten that they are made in the image of God. "And he made them drink water of forgetfulness . . . in order that they might not know from where they came." John, in the midst of tears, hears Christ say that he is the memory of what humans have forgotten. Later, in the *Acts of John,* Christ says, "I am a lamp to you who see me, I am a mirror to you who perceive, I am a door to you who knock on me, I am a way to you, wayfarer." Thinking of this as I make my way across the rocky terrain, I'm curious about how the Celts came to believe something so similar to John's dream—their conviction that Christ came to remind us of our origins in God. I'm drawn to the idea of Christ the awakener, Christ the mirror, Christ the memory, and I feel the truth of it deep inside me.

I'm reminded then that what makes Iona special—both to the ancient Celts and to modern-day pilgrims—is its reputation as a "thin place," a spot where people feel a powerful connection to God's presence, where the veils between the worlds part just enough to allow us a glimpse of something beyond. *Are these veils what blind us to a deeper reality? Are they what keep us from seeing our origins in God, from remembering who we are?*

Suddenly I remember being in a church in France several years ago watching a man sitting nearby. After a minute or so, I noticed he had whatever disorder makes people continually move in strange ways. His particular tic was one in which he seemed to be constantly wiping away cobwebs from his face, his head, his arms, and legs. The movements were graceful, and in the brief moments between them, he was composed and thoughtful-looking. Watching him, you could begin to believe there really were veils of some kind he was dusting aside—you could almost see them—because his movements were so full of grace and intent, and each time he made a move, it seemed new, not just a habitual series of actions. I tried to imagine a lifetime of this constant movement, and how exhausting it might be for him to keep chasing away the veils that only he could see.

Only a few walkers remain when we reach the top of the cliff overlooking Columba's Bay. My fellow pilgrims walk on without me, and I sit in silence to take in the beauty. The sky is overcast now and there's a sense of being enveloped by the dense clouds. I make a conscious effort to breathe the air and feel the cool ground beneath me. I study the shape of the clouds and the slope of the land. I listen to the wind, feel it lift the hair from my neck. I hear the waves in the distance. Without warning, the world stops, and there's not a sound. Everything changes before my eyes. The cliff, the stones on the beach, the sandy incline, the sea and the sky are alive, humming with a deep and potent presence. The world feels small and boundless at the same time, and I feel the hidden heart that beats beneath every living thing. Picking up a stone, I notice it shines with the colors of the sea, the texture of the earth, the warmth of the sun, and the shape of the world. *There's only presence now at what feels like the heart of the everything, and I'm soaring, only in stillness, without movement. I sit for a long time, allowing the humming energy and presence to surround and fill me.*

THAT NIGHT, I DREAM. In the dream, I see Christ standing with a group in a circle. I enter the circle and try to touch his shoulder to see if he's real. The group begins to dance, and then I am standing beside Christ. He leans his forehead to touch mine, and when I open one eye to peek, I do not see his face; instead I see my own face looking back at me.

In the dance I find you,
and touch your shoulder lightly,
trailing slowly, watchful, mute,
as you gather us in threads of brightness.

Drawn by your rhythm, your words,
I move round you in the circle
'til we meet and pause,
in a moment, an eternity of presence.

You lean to touch your face to mine,
your shadow and your light so near,
but stepping back, I see my own image there,
an invisible glass between us
returns lost pieces of a shining self.

I keep still, searching to know
beyond the names others use to claim you,
but I hear only the song you sing to me
in the shimmering silence.

You are the memory of the me who was lost,
the one scattered to the years and days,
given back now in the fierce light
of your tender, loving gaze.

MELANIE S. BAFFES, a writer, editor, and book developer, has worked in the field of publishing for more than twenty-five years and is founder of Hidden Wholeness, a publishing group that develops manuals, guidebooks, and educational programs for nonprofit institutions. She is working on a collection of travel essays about finding the sacred in out-of-the-way places while she pursues a master's degree in divinity at a Chicago seminary.

Directions to You

Here I come—
Like the Tom, Dick & Harrys who went before,
My notes scribbled on a cable bill, wet
Next to the Piggly Wiggly flowers on the seat.

You said take the Central Freeway, head north,
Keep going, past downtown,
Past what I know, 'til I come to the first exit that feels right.
Get on the access, turn left at the light.

Follow that road through several miles of detours and deconstruction
Then, any time after the Exxon, hand Whimsy the wheel—
Left or right—you named your cat Kismet,
And "Fate needs to be riding shotgun on this."

Now follow the two lane macadam to the third intersection.
Men, one old, one late middle-aged will be playing checkers.
The tall one will rise, approach, kick the tires, talk weather,
And if he points, persist in that direction for a mile and a half.

There will be a series of streets named after authors.
Choose the one that was a better poet than novelist, turn left.
This is the street. And the house.
The house was described in detail two nights before.

Above all else you want a man that listens, really listens.

BRUCE NELSON has been writing on and off for a number of years while teaching. He has taught from the college to the elementary level. He and his wife recently moved to Austin, Texas, where he is an elementary school principal. Nelson says, "Writing for me is a passion, a release. It makes me watch life more closely. In fact, I write a lot of my poems in the car. 'Directions to You' was written during a car trip to Dallas to see a friend."

Rooster

ROOSTER HAD DRUNK PLUMB THROUGH HIS PAYCHECK the night before and could hardly see straight, let alone follow this dang map he was holding. He'd found it in his pocket when he woke up in his beach-side trailer that morning. Scrawled in pencil, the hand-drawn map had a girl's name on it: "Sue."

Oh my God, he'd thought, *what'd I do now?* He searched his wallet for clues, finding none. All it held was his driver's license, some maxed-out credit cards, an expired contractor's license, and his paycheck stub. Not a greenback in sight. There were some poker IOU's, but his card buddies were deadbeats. They never paid up. Then he remembered his rent was due. He moaned and dragged his lanky six-foot frame into the bathroom. "I've gone about as low as a gopher in a coal mine," he said to the mirror.

But later, after he'd showered and shaved, thrown on a crumpled pair of 501s, and had a cup of black coffee with a pinch of whiskey— nothing like the hair of the dog that bit 'cha—he thought he'd see where the map took him.

"Hey Tallulah, what you think? Shall we go for a look-see?" Rooster jumped into the cab of his beat-up pickup, leaning his back against the seat while the standard poodle leapt over and took her place next to him on the bench, sitting upright with her shaggy white forepaws braced in front of her. Nothing Tallulah loved more than a Sunday drive. Rooster gunned the engine and headed out of the foggy coastal town toward the Santa Cruz foothills.

Forty minutes later, map in hand, squinting at the sun, his brain pressing against his skull like hot cotton, and some idiot honking behind him, Rooster was about to quit. He hadn't a clue where to go next, and the shady bar down by the beach looked better than any dame.

Right then, Tallulah looked over at him with a grin—open jaw dripping with happy drool, swinging her head to the side, long flaps of ears following, letting out a bark of excitement. That's when he saw it—the road he'd been searching for. Just past that little stone bridge ahead was the marker, "Trout Gulch." The one-lane road was rough and rocky as could be.

He passed an old brown barn, then a little white house with children's playthings out front, rusted and faded against the stubbled volunteer grass that served as lawn. He hardly noticed. It was all junk to him. He cared not a whit for the well-groomed chestnut horse that shook its mane and whinnied as he drove by. That only made Rooster's head hurt. Then Tallulah barked with a frenzy at the horse and oh, he could hardly bear the hammering that caused. He stepped on the gas and tore past the cedar A-frame house on the left, insulted by the "SLOW DOWN—EXCESSIVE DUST!" sign that had been hand-lettered and nailed to the trunk of a tree nearby. "Serves 'em right," he thought. "Who the hell are they to tell me!"

Suddenly the road narrowed. Tall redwoods towered on either side, ages old, dwarfing the pickup and its inhabitants. Tallulah stopped barking, sitting still as stone and staring out the windshield. The pounding in his head quieted. The dust settled. He slowed the truck to a crawl, looking at the trees, leaning his head out the window. Tallulah did the same. He felt as though he had entered another world, hushed and magical. The ancient majesty of the trees moved him to unexpected reverence. Tallulah felt it too, quietly whimpering, pressing her curly head against her forepaws, then cozying up beside him. Finally he let the car come to a halt, shutting down the engine. The two of them just sat there, alone with the silence, soaking it in.

Gradually Rooster began to notice the fine-needled redwood fronds lift and sway to an invisible breeze, like dancing. One tree in particular caught his attention. It stood in a small clearing, reaching above the others. Slants of light illumined its scattered branches. He got out of his truck, leaving the door ajar so as not to break the silence, moving one quiet foot at a time, Tallulah with him, to get a better look. There he stood; leathery neck craned back to take in the height of the tall redwood. _My God,_ he thought, _how beautiful._ His spirit hushed. Tallulah lay down, chin resting on her forepaws, nose tucked between.

Rooster saw now with his heart as much as his eyes, transfixed, becoming aware of a graciousness to this tree, a patience and strength. He thought how it had stood here through the centuries, providing home to the life that found shelter in its branches, forgiving the civilization that relentlessly encroached. He thought of the

patience it took to do that, and the love. *How sweet you are,* he said within himself.

"*Sometimes sorrow stands in your path like sentinels, blocking the way to the path that leads home.*"

"Where'd that come from?" Rooster thought. He turned his head to the side, as if someone had said it to him, but the voice was inside him. He stared at the tree.

"*What took you so long?*" came that voice again, tenderly. "*What took you so long?*"

Then, like a slow, quiet lullaby within him, came this. "*Let it go, let it go. Life has its sorrows, let them all go.*"

Rooster sat down on the forest floor, cross-legged, head bowed, eyes closed, while the words repeated themselves, sinking like stones to the core of him. Tallulah sat beside, not making a move. Time slowed, minutes deep as hours.

Images colored the darkness: birthday parties, fishing trips, summers down by the river of his youth; his dad taking him fishing, teaching him how to cast his rod so the fly would dance on the sunlit water; playing hide and seek with the neighbor kids in the hay barn, climbing the stacks, swinging down from the top on the rope that hung from the crossbeams; showing his little sister his secret place to hide; his mother calling them in to supper, the clang of the cowbell she rang.

Margit Varga.
Connecticut Farm.
Oil on board,
19½ x 29½ in., 1938.
Collection of The
University of Arizona
Museum of Art, Tucson.
Gift of C. Leonard Pfeiffer.
Photograph by Peter
Balestrero.

He wanted those images to stay, but new ones took their place: his mother at the stove, tears in her eyes, ladling soup into bowls; his father tousling his head, leaning down, kissing him goodbye; his sister running after, grabbing at the tall man's legs; the man setting her gently aside, turning away, hopping into the truck, the smell of exhaust trailing behind.

Then again, *"Let it go, let it go. Life has its sorrows, let them all go."* He sank deeper still, till it seemed he'd never come back.

EVENTUALLY A SQUIRREL RAN PAST TALLULAH. The dog took chase, barks piercing the silence. Rooster jerked to his feet, a diver pulled from the depths of the sea.

He turned to the tree, but the spell was broken.

"Hey, Ta'Loo! Don't go chasin' after squirrels," he called with a smile. "C'mon, Girl, hop in the truck." The dog climbed in and Rooster followed, starting the engine. They drove another quarter mile, redwood giving way to pine and fir, the lower trunks of these choked in ivy ropes of green.

Up the road ahead Rooster saw a ragged row of mailboxes, all different colors and shapes. One stood out. It was painted burgundy red. Stenciled across the side in green block letters was "868 Trout Gulch," just like the map said. It had a flag up.

Rooster looked around to see what house went with the mailbox but saw none, so he kept on going. Around the bend was an apple orchard, unkempt and let go. One tree, limbs hoary with lichen and moss, stood apart, just a single red burst of fruit hanging from its silvered branches. To the right, the orchard unfolded across a sloped pasture, ripened fruit spilt in puddles on the soft ground, yellow, red and brown. Yellow jackets buzzed here and there, seeking the warm sweet juice. Wild grass cluttered the spaces between the trees, making a bed for a long gray cat, stretched out on his side in the sun. The land rolled down to a green wooded wall, solid with bush and bramble, hinting of a ravine beyond. *Trout Gulch!* he thought.

"Look at that, Ta'Loo! Did you ever see anything so beautiful?" Once again, he pulled the car to the side of the road, shut down the engine, and jumped out. Finding the orchard irresistible, he forgot about the girl he'd come to find. On the orchard floor, silent, the two of them, man and dog, sat down, Tallulah not even growling at the cat.

Out of the blue, Rooster quietly began to weep. "Babe," he said, throwing his long arm around the gawky dog, "I don't know what's come over me. Like to died when my daddy left, you know that?" He paused, as if for her answer. Tallulah turned her head, looking at him. "All those years, waiting, watching the road for his truck. He never came." He rubbed the dog behind her ears. "Now I feel like I've come home to my momma's farm. No more watching. No more waiting." Resentment drained out like battery acid.

He began to think about his life, how he'd thrown it away on whiskey, drugs, high-heeled women, and cards; barely scraping by with nowhere jobs, always a chip on his shoulder. He felt ashamed, amazed, and renewed; all at the same time.

"Oh my goodness, who do we have here?"

Startled, Rooster turned to find a tall attractive woman standing over him, holding a basket full of apples against her waist. "May I help you?" she asked.

Rooster looked up, shading his eyes with his hand. She was blonde, hair pulled back in a ponytail, wearing a white T-shirt and faded khaki shorts, bare limbs tan against them. "Uh, we were just resting a bit, Ma'am—didn't mean any harm." Rooster stumbled to his feet while Tallulah wagged her tail and sniffed the woman's ankles. "I'm Jasper, Jasper Johnson. Most people call me Rooster though, 'cause my hair's so red. And this is Tallulah." He blushed, grabbing the dog's collar, feeling shy as a schoolboy. "Have we met?" he asked hesitantly, as he extended his free hand.

The woman shifted the apple basket to her hip and took his hand. "No, I don't think so," she said. "Sue. Sue Olsen. How do you do?"

He remembered the name on the map. He turned bright red, the tiny hairs standing out on the back of his neck. He winced inside himself at the thought of his blacked-out night before.

"You weren't at a party last night down by the beach, were you? . . . Old Jake's bar? I live near there." Rooster pulled out the scrap of paper with the map and name scrawled on it, showing it to her.

"Nope, that's not my writing. Looks like my brother's though. Sent you here, did he?"

"Sort of," he said, shoving the paper in his pocket.

"Well, Jasper," she said. "I've just made some lemonade for my neighbors. They're coming over to do a little fly-fishing down by the stream, behind my place. They say you can see the trout jump clear as day, even from my back porch. Sun's just at the right angle. Would you and Tallulah like to join us?"

She turned toward a small white house, set deep against the woods, flat-roofed, its backside to the road. He hadn't noticed it before. He just nodded, speechless.

Tallulah took off toward the house, prancing like leading a parade. Sue and Jasper followed.

"You wouldn't happen be a fly fisher, would you?" she asked as they walked. "My dad was a big catch and release fan. He got me a rod." She paused, crossing her arms, holding herself close, looking away. "I'd just gone through a pretty rocky divorce. Dad thought it would help. But he was gone before he had a chance to teach me. Died in his sleep, no warning. Thought my heart would break. Sometimes I think it did." She looked back at him.

"I . . . I . . ." Rooster tried to answer, but only a croak came out.

"You think you could teach me?" she asked.

Finally, Rooster found his voice. "I . . . I'd love to. Least give it a try. My daddy taught me to fly-fish when I was a kid. Funny, I was thinking of him when you walked up." He stared past her for a moment at the redwoods that lined the gulch. "We used to fish together, up north along the Truckee." He looked at her then, stopping there in the field, just short of the house. "Some things you never forget." He paused, silent for a heartbeat. "Now, what'd you say about lemonade and good company? Can't think of anything better for a Sunday afternoon."

ELLEN O'NEILL is a career consultant to job seekers in Silicon Valley. Her feature stories have appeared in several newspapers, including the *Christian Science Monitor*. She lives in Santa Cruz County, not far from the sea, off a dirt and gravel road much like the one Rooster discovers in this story. This is her debut publication in fiction.

RICHARD N. BENTLEY

Hallowe'en Afternoon

A small town, the store windows
Decorated with gravestones,
Witches, pumpkins,
ghosts
Paint
                    Streaking down
                              the glass
                                   In the rain.
A little girl dressed as
A rabbit, led across the street
By her mother,
Under an umbrella.
Have you ever stopped
To listen to the rain
In the lapse of a quarrel?
It means the quarrel will end.
It means you can see
The pavement on which the rain falls, and
The complexity of wet leaves
On it, curved leaves,
Flattened leaves.
The girl dressed as a rabbit
And her mother
Stop in front of an old
House with red shutters.
A chicken opens the door.

RICHARD N. BENTLEY is a graduate of Yale University and the Vermont College Writing Program. His recent books of poems and short stories, *Post-Freudian Dreaming* and *A General Theory of Desire* are available from amazon.com or www.dickbentley.com. He was a winner of the *Paris Review/ Paris Writers Workshop* International Fiction Award in 1994. He teaches at Mount Holyoke College.

Walking by the Rectory

Charles Ephraim
Burchfield.
Sulphurous Evening.
Watercolor on paper
mounted on board,
23⅜ x 25 ⁵/₁₆ in.,
1922–1929.
Saint Louis Art Museum.
Eliza McMillan Trust.

I'M BACK IN MY HOMETOWN, in fact, or, in imagination ... the distinction is not always clear. It's late and cold and dark, and it's December, and I scurry by St. Andrews and look up at the gold-colored cross, and it occurs to me that I have somehow misplaced thirty years. I frown at the darkened, leaden windows.

I never linger passing any Catholic church. We who grew up as frank Baptists, thinking priests Rome clones whose old, worn-shiny black robes were infested with the dust of papal-blackened magic, always scurried by. Priests were a bit alarming, but at least, you never saw one on the street. They did not frequent public thoroughfares but

28

lived in ancient, eighteen-room rectories made of brick or stone or some fortress-fit material, kept clean and warm by a devout and stern, bone-thin Irish/Italian woman who cooked outrageous dinners of roast beef and roast potatoes, and cakes with rum and brandy.

The rectories had standard-issue table lamps placed dead center in front of every window, so that walking by, in half light, half shivers, half hunger, half despair, the place looked the very picture of a heaven. Those yellow lights dredged longing from your protesting soul for never-visited, forgotten, still-remembered things. That's what the lights were for, to make you long to be a Catholic in a thick, warm coat with thick, warm soup steaming on the stove and smelling of the tartest tarragon, the heartiest potato, and powerful brown bread, and overflowing flasks of purple grape communion wine. Lights like that could make one go to catechism five afternoons a week.

I walked by this rectory two times a day for all the years that memory was casting experience in stone, and the edifice did not fail, not one time, to capture my attention.

I walk on by in failing light tonight and think I will avert my eyes. But it's no good. The bricks are magnetized. They'd draw my gaze if I were blind. I study the structure like a puzzle to decipher. I stop, arrested by a little, cold-sounding, noisy click, exaggerated by the holy silence that the night forbears to break, now settling down around the holy house.

A priest. On the front stoop. He bends to pick up the newspaper. I thought a priest would have a housekeeper to bring the paper in, unfold it, press it, maybe with an iron. On low.

When I was a child, if a priest needed a pocket comb, I assumed he never went himself, but sent a nun to do the shopping. How else explain the frequent sightings of nuns, who with unsettling regularity cruised the aisles of 5&10s and pharmacies.

Their long black habits, sad, deserted faces, menacing in ways a burly priest could never be. Even I, who could only tell for certain who was Catholic, who was not, by looking at their saddle oxford shoes— black and white sold just to Protestants, brown and white to baptized members of the holy Roman Mother Church — knew nuns were somehow fierce and capable beyond all reason. I wanted nothing to do with them and was always more than reassured to see the woman hanging out the sheets beside the rectory was not done up in thin, black, silky clothes.

I give a little shudder. The priest holding the newspaper on the porch in the December night turns and lifts the creaky mailbox lid to take out one slim bit of mail, perhaps a letter from another priest who's lost his faith—the second time this year—perhaps only a reminder from his dentist.

He looks down the letter and then raises his eyes and stares out at the night.

Just in case.

He lifts his chin.

Dear God in Heaven. Holy Mary Mother of God, I would say if I were Catholic. It's David Thomas, or if it's not, it is a balding priest who's got his face.

David Thomas, Dave Tom. Davey Tommy. Wavey Davey. Tom the Bomb. I went to school with him. We went to the same church. A hundred days a week. The same *BAPTIST* church that fervently and vocally believed the only worse thing than the devil was the Pope. We had it straight from John, that first and most emphatic Baptist.

So how did Davey Thomas catapult his eternally-saved self from the water tank beneath our altar at First Baptist, to the Holy Roman Church, and not just as a fly-by-night confessor but as a well-nourished man of the cloth, complete with collar, black clothes, and a twelve-room rectory.

"Hello," he calls out. Even his voice is Davey Thomas's.

I start and realize I've been standing, frozen, freezing, in one spot, and staring. I'm not infrequently surprised to tune back in and discover what my body has been up to while my mind has been off on a Disney cruise. Plus I always feel the slightest bit invisible.

"Hello," I say. We study one another.

At least he doesn't ask if he can help me. He hasn't grown that pompous yet.

"I like December," he calls out.

I hate it. Not the month itself, only the Christmas part which does all but hog the whole thing.

"Your mother loved December," I reply in a soft voice.

"What?" he says as he starts down the stairs, each careful step assuring me I need not raise my voice, that he will come as close as need be. I can whisper if I want.

"Your mother loved December," I say again.

"I know," he says, "And your mum despised it. In fact, I can't remember a month she did like."

"You recognize me." I am surprised. I had my nose fixed in my twenties, and my acne's gone. I've put on thirty needless pounds, and had my teeth capped, and my hair is a new, close-cropped strawberry blond—fruit red in certain light.

"Of course I recognize you. I'm a priest, not an idiot."

I'd be a whole lot less surprised were it the other way around.

So how did it happen, I want to ask, but I can't get from where I am to any phrasing short of cheeky rude. How on earth did they ever let a Baptist be a priest? *What possessed them?* my mother would have said. In my mother's book, you stuck to your own kind and everybody knew where everybody was. A Baptist priest, no use to them and none to us.

He points to his dog collar like he's shooting it. "You're probably wondering where I got these clothes."

"I figured Rome," I say.

"Vatican City Fine Menswear."

That's another thing about a Catholic. They're so precise.

"You're cold out here," Davey says. "Come in." He points to the holy fortress and does a little jig-jog step, and we are seven-year-old kids, double-dog daring one another up the walk, with taunts and jibes and shrieks and shoves. *"I dare you." "I double dare you." "Pope, Pope on a rope." "Nuns, nuns, they have guns."* Until finally, emboldened by the darkness and the cold that in the end is only wearying, we grab hands and run together up and touch the railing on the porch, and turn and run, till we are heaving, out of breath, and late at night, will lie awake and wonder, long after all the nuns in town are fast asleep, wonder is it possible we have contracted some papal disease, committed some unpardonable Protestant sin. We're not afraid of Catholic punishment, with no hope of pardon for our trespasses—which only Presbyterians, and certain Methodists, implore *"Our Father"* to *"forgive."* We pray forgive us our *debts* as we forgive our *debtors* and would be entirely satisfied with that.

We're not afraid of *them.* We are afraid of *us.* "Don't tell the preacher," we whisper to each other the next day at school.

"Come in," Davey says. "Come on in."

"We can't," I say. "I mean, I can't. You can't be bringing women in."

"I'm not about to *have my way* with you. I'm offering you a cup of tea or sherry, unless that's still a sin."

"No, sherry's fine."

"Well, come then. I'll show you around."

What? Doesn't he know what he's doing? Can he not remember? He stands here, on this Wednesday, in old, cold December, and he threatens to fulfill a wish I've carried around alive with me for fifty years.

Come in, he says, just like that. *Here, have a million dollars. Here, be twenty-two again and three full inches taller. Here, marry this movie star we have for you.*

I move on stick-stiff legs with Davey up the walk. I'm going to my coronation. The audience has clapped the loudest and the longest for my story. I'm *Queen for a Day.* I am condemned. My legs now carry me, against my will, to my certain execution.

Davey pulls open the heavy door, I think perhaps a bit self-consciously, but am in no state to judge, when at the moment, I could well mistake a flicker for a bolt of lightning.

"Here, let me take your coat," Davey says.

I need it, it's holding me together, I don't say. "I can only stay for a minute," I say instead.

Somehow I would have expected to be greeted by a parlor maid, petite, decked out in an Art-Deco-age, black rayon, under a white, complicated apron, wearing a white frilly cap. But, we are quite alone.

I'd like to stand here, in this foyer, for an hour, take it in, then come back every afternoon and do a different room. At the same time I would like to run from room to room like a crazy person, panting, gushing, slipping on the Catholic, oriental rugs. I'd like to go back home, and get my stuff, and move right in, and stay forever. Davey could sneak me in and out at night for exercise. I could grow old and die here, and the ochre, ochre walls would never tell. Davey and I could drive to West Virginia after years of long companionship—if not desire—and marry, make it all right in the sight of God, if not the Catholic church. The two are not the same. But you knew that.

Or I could run out to the pantry, trip the housekeeper as she crosses the kitchen carrying six ramekins of custard in a pan of boiling water from the oven to the counter, visit her daily in the burn ward of the local hospital, then take her job as penance—something Baptists are more practiced at than might be generally believed.

Or, they might discharge the housekeeper from the Catholic hospital, scars healed and hardly showing. It could be a miracle. And I could come and live here, not to wash and iron and scrub but to be washed and ironed and scrubbed for.

"What would you like to see first?" Davey says.

"The cellar." My honest reply. It's a matter of *not wanting* the best too soon. It's eating the crust before the filling. Aging a new dress in the closet for six months. Getting all A's for sixteen years in a row before you take a day off school to watch two movies in a row.

"I don't recommend the basement," Davey says. "Lots of little rooms that must have once been torture chambers, during the Pennsylvania inquisition, noisy plumbing, dust, and mice."

Davey leads me room to room. He's nine years old and showing me his castle, sneaking peeks to see my wonderment. That, or I am lying sprawled across his narrow twin bed, in the sorry room he shares with his twin sister, Julie Ann, my best friend, while he's out playing stick ball. We lie here planning lives that are far, far too big for anybody from this town. This bedroom, their whole house, is a nightmare. Even the preacher's wife says somebody should torch the thing and start again, and she is a resourceful woman. Davey's and Julie Ann's mother, a woman who once had a nervous breakdown, lies on the davenport downstairs, and clutter and a sad disorder overrun the place.

Julie Ann has a small, beat-up bureau she keeps tidy, with a limp doily weighted with a jewelry box, home to a wounded ballerina, with a King James Bible lying on top. But it's an aberration in this musty-smelling house, where misery and grime have won out long ago.

Each room Davey shows me is pristine in twelve different, Catholic ways. It may be the one experience of my life that offers me no disappointment. It is a Catholic house in the same way the house where Davey and Julie Ann grew up was Baptist, pure and simple, far beyond human redemption, dependent entirely and forever on the grace of God and Jesus's mercy. This rectory is self-sufficient. It hardly needs a God at all. Its walls are sturdy, flanked by cherry hardwood worn to rich patina. It is a house to run to in the storm.

Not quite the house where you grew up, I want to say to Davey, but something happens, when you turn eighteen, that makes that sort of sentence stop at your puckered lips, phrased to pose, but never said.

"You live here all alone?" I say.

"I know. I know," he says. "You're thinking people sleep out on the street, and I have fourteen rooms." It's obvious he's counted. "Not a heck of a whole lot like the place where we grew up."

Heck. That's Baptist. A born Catholic would say hell or not say anything.

"Whatever happened to Julie Ann?" I say.

"Nothing happened." He speaks like that's my fault. "She lives over in the flats. She has five kids, a hundred grandkids, and a husband that's a wicked drunk."

I do not think it ever once occurred to me, sprawled out on Davey's wire-spring bed, daydreaming in concert with Julie Ann, that she and Davey would grow up and have entire, lived lives. It isn't that I thought that they would die, so much as that they would just fade away, growing less distinct with time, and, one day, be no more. And here Davey is, as big as all religion, walking room to room in all his priestly pleasure causing me to wonder can it be that everyone I ever knew went on to have a whole life, after I forgot them. I would need a full year by the calendar to sit and devise fantasies of the particulars of that.

"Julie Ann's sinkhole of a husband never works, he's been in jail three times."

"Oh my." I feel so guilty. Julie Ann and I were friends, real friends right up till junior high, when I got put in all the smart-kid classes.

Me and Davey. I should have kept better track of her. I could have told her to break up the first time she went out with the bad husband. What am I saying? Davey could have had her and the five kids come live with him and grow up here.

"Is she Catholic too?" I say.

"No."

"How about your mother?"

"She's not Catholic either."

"No, I mean is she still here?"

"No, she moved with some guy to Florida the year that I converted. She never budged off the sofa all the years that we were growing up, and then we graduated, and she moved a thousand miles away. She said she wouldn't be able to hold her head up when she went to the BY-LO for groceries, that everybody and his brother would know she was the mother of a full-blown priest, with my long black robes billowing out behind my fat bum as I walked down the street. She said she could no longer show her face in town; she'd have to find a new church somewhere else where no one knew her."

Frankly I'm impressed she had the energy to say all that.

I try to remember Davey's dad, but he's not there to be summoned.

Then suddenly I realize that Davey and I are no longer alone. In the dim light, I can just make out that invalid, in-valid mother of his, over in the corner on the antique, horsehair sofa, underneath the gleaming crucifix. She has, she tells us, devoted the entire month of December to one headache. She does not even open up her eyes. But it's not just this mother who has now appeared. I look through the shadows and there sits Julie Ann, a young girl, perched on the edge of a straight-backed chair, wearing her very finest, her hair in dreadful curls that she is just young and pretty enough to carry off. I can hardly take it in.

And then, just like that, who walks in, but Jesus. I recognize Him in a heartbeat. I'd heard a key in the back door and thought it was the housekeeper.

Jesus looks around. Julie Ann's a very sweet thirteen, I'm fifty-seven, Davey's ageless, the aggrieved mother is asleep, but none of this will be a problem.

"So, you're all here," Jesus says, like the one who called the meeting. I hope he's gearing up to tell the mother *Rise, take up your bed and walk, and make these kids some supper.* I hope he's here to give us all do-overs, but I know that's not what mercy is. The mother sleeps on. (You have to get yourself up off the horsehair sofa if you want the blessing. That's the deal.)

Jesus grins at Davey, reaches out and takes a little bit of cloth— *the* cloth—between two callused fingers.

"Nice threads," He says.

Why, He's not pissed at all that Davey is a Catholic. He winks at me and reaches in his pocket and pulls out a little box he hands to me.

"What's this?" I say.

"Those thirty years that you misplaced," he says. "I hope you like what I have done with them."

The air feels like the air that California redwoods make.

"Well, let's get this show on the road," he says, and rubs his hands together, and we are all entirely willing to fall in with any plan he might propose.

Just then Julie Ann's five children parade in, followed by their own children, and a boy who will surely grow to be the man that Julie Ann will one day marry. Everybody's some age different from their real age now, that is, except for Davey and me.

"Maggie. You're just fine the way you are." Jesus has just read my thoughts.

And suddenly, with him standing here, I want to confess all my sins, *be washed white as snow.*

"I am mean," I blurt out. "Really mean inside my heart."

"I know," he says and smiles.

"I'm temperamental and fussy and controlling, and I seem to bring out the worst in people."

"That's good," he says. "I want the worst out. You bring it out, I'll sweep it away. We're a good team."

And the angels cry out *Holy, holy, holy is the Lord,* and Davey says, "I'm really sorry too."

"I know," Jesus says. "I know that. What's got into everybody here?"

And then he leads us all out to the dining room, where a hundred candles burn and where the table holds a mighty feast and where we sit till after midnight telling stories, remembering together, Jesus filling in the parts we didn't know. Turns out he's got the real skinny on everything that's ever happened in our lives.

"I guess it's not like what you thought." Davey and I are standing in the library. I'm putting on my coat. "The rectory, I mean."

"Oh no," I say. "It's wonderful. It's better than I ever dreamed."

"You probably think it's terrible that I became a priest," he says.

"Oh no, I think it's wonderful. I do. And Jesus does too."

"You think?" he says.

"I know," I say.

Five minutes more and I am back out standing on the street. When I left, Davey headed back toward the dining room. I'm guessing he and Jesus weren't quite finished with each other yet.

I stand here on the sidewalk. The wind whips at the pavement grit and sand, but I'm not cold. In the rectory, in the room I calculate to be the library, some Irish/Italian woman—who in this light looks more Scandinavian than anything—turns on the yellow table lamp. I stand and watch as one by one the lights go on in all the yellow table lamps in all the rooms. And so, was she, like me, one time a child who stood outside at night when it was cold?

Nothing's changed. Or certainly nothing that hasn't changed a million times before. It's just that here, tonight, several things were possible for a few minutes, all at the same time. It reminds me that long ago, any number of remembered and forgotten times, whole lifetimes of things were possible, and I am standing far too near the Catholic church to believe, not for dead certain, that things could never be that possible again.

I start to walk away, puzzled, not sure at all. Did I see Davey Thomas come out on the porch tonight to get the newspaper, and did he ask me in, and be the priest, and tell me all about his mother, and Julie Ann, and her sorry excuse for a husband, or did I just imagine it? Did Davey really walk me room to room, remembering with me? Did Jesus come in, by the back door, and smile at us and tell us he was able and entirely willing, even this late in the day, to make the whole damn thing okay?

I don't think I could have made that last part up.

LINDA MCCULLOUGH MOORE, author of *The Distance Between* (Soho Press), is published in more than two hundred publications and currently has a novel and a short story collection in search of a good home.

RICK KEMPA

At Spirit Lake

I shed my clothes
and stand at the water's edge.
I tell myself that when I move

I will not be timid—
suffering each small step,
dreading the immersion—

but with a headlong plunge
will enter
that other element.

In truth, I do not want to.
I want the sun
warm upon my skin,

this feathery wind,
my firm footing in the sand
to not end.

But because a young man
stood on this same edge once,
yearning to be clean,

yearning, he thought,
to leave behind
everyone and everything,

to know the world so fully that
his bones burned
and his heart was seized,

because he was not able
to leave his safe ground
and believed later

that he had failed,
that he was less than
he was meant to be,

because the shadows lengthen
at the pool's edge,
because there is no safe ground,

I plunge.

Poet, essayist, and inveterate hiker, RICK KEMPA lives in Rock Springs, Wyoming, where he directs the honors program at Western Wyoming College. His student, Liesel Shineberg, as he says, "a young eighty-year-old," has won the Swedenborg Foundation's annual Baily Prize for prose. Her story on an ultimate renewal, "The Metzger Brothers," begins on page 174.

II. Regeneration

LAURENCE HOLDEN

Working Clay

for Lynn

Out of the loins of the bin
we claw and scoop
clay up

gather its body
to our aproned chest

carry its soddened weight
sticky, slippery,
glistening as afterbirth

to a table
to make pots.

We unearth the dead
to make again,
to remake, refigure

a shape once sought:
just this way against that

just so,
foot, body, lip,
root, rind, flower

worked trim
worked polished

but I think figured
in the grain of this
something else:

just how the stars orbit
just how our hearts hurt.

LAURENCE HOLDEN draws from his daily experience in living along
Warwoman Creek in the North Georgia mountains to paint and to write
poetry. This poem is dedicated to his wife.

DAVID S. RUBENSTEIN

Resurrection Bingo

FOR ALMOST A DECADE, I had made a weekly trek from Chicago to Chillicothe, always taking the same highway, flying past the same rural landscapes in a blur of inattention, cell phone implanted in ear, Blackberry buzzing beside me. It wasn't until spring of the tenth year, when the Illinois River bolted the caution of its banks and submerged a startled interstate that I was spit out of the major artery into a narrow capillary of patched and meandering asphalt.

After exiting the highway in a procession of irritated drivers flagged off by state troopers, I drove the two-lane road that clung to the riparian ridge, floating along with the power line waves that rose and fell between wooden poles like a gentle sea. Ahead, on a hillock with a commanding view of the river valley, rose a small brownstone church no different from the many others that I passed on the trip, its pointed hat rising above a copse of trees and protecting army of gravestone soldiers. When I crested the rise just before it, I came upon a chaos of vehicles parked haphazardly along both shoulders. Cars were stopped in the road to jockey for parking places. People walked from all directions along and in the road toward the church, bundled against the cold, their breaths escaping in visible puffs, oblivious to the clotted traffic.

I tried to control my impatience as I attempted to make my way down the road, ensnared like a car in the highlands of Scotland entirely surrounded by sheep. Ahead, on a weathered marquee sign in the yard in front of the church, in red letters over a white background, were the words "Resurrection Bingo." Beneath, in smaller letters read "This year, March 4."

As I threaded my way through the crowd, I noticed that it was not comprised solely of little old ladies looking to be on their way to a church social. There were adults of all ages, mostly alone, occasionally in pairs, looking solemn and determined. They did not look at all like what I envisioned as a typical church bingo crowd.

Curious, I lowered the window and asked a middle-aged man walking at the same speed I was driving, "What's up with this bingo?"

He glanced over at me and responded, without breaking stride, "Resurrection Bingo."

When it was obvious he was not going to elaborate, I asked, "Does it always draw such a crowd?"

"Yes." And he turned off the road toward the entrance.

It was then that I began to notice the license plates on the cars parked along the road. Plenty of Illinois plates to be sure, but many out-of-state plates too. Seemed like more than half. By the time I passed the church and cleared the congestion, I knew I'd have to see what was going on.

I pulled off onto the shoulder, soft and damp with the recent rains, hoping I'd be able to get back onto the road. Checking my side-view mirror for traffic, I opened the door, struggled out against the tilt of the car, and transformed myself from the role of aggrieved motorist into part of the problem.

Following the crowd, I entered a side door of the church and descended a scalloped flight of well-worn stairs. The basement was a single, large room filled with tables and chairs. And people. More people than I had anticipated. More, I'm certain, than the fire marshall would have allowed. But, other than the sounds of movement, of chairs being drawn back or up, of coughs or of creaks, it had the quiet of a church service. The faint smell of disinfectant was discernable within the common odor of bodies and damp coats. The faded ceiling tiles, stained brown in places from leaks past and present, seemed to press down on the crowd. "Bad idea," I thought, and turned back toward the door. But my attention was drawn to a queue before a table at the side of the room where a sign declared "Bingo Cards, $10 each. Limit one per person."

When in Rome, I mentally shrugged, and joined the line. When I reached the front, I handed a woman a ten-dollar bill and received a bingo card. I turned to find a seat.

The people on either side of me did not speak or acknowledge me as I sat. Most of them had a photograph on the table in front of them. I took surreptitious peeks at them. Some were wallet-sized, bent, and frayed as though they had been carried for years. Others were larger, standing in ornate frames before their owners, all of whom seemed to be fingering or speaking to them. A low undertone of murmuring could be heard, and many lips moved silently.

In the center of the table was a bowl of buttons. Everyone had taken some, presumably to mark their cards. I reached in and withdrew a handful, which I placed on the table in front of me. I noticed immediately that my pile seemed bigger than that of everyone else. Seemed as though everyone else had only about five buttons. No, everyone had exactly five buttons. I immediately felt self-conscious, like some kind of button-hoarder. But there seemed to be plenty left in the bowl, so I let it pass.

The room became deathly still when a man walked up to the front table. He was a tall, gaunt man, dressed in black, with a white clerical collar. His face was etched with wear, but I couldn't tell if from age or experience. Without a word, he turned the crank on a barrel containing Bingo tiles. All eyes were on him as he opened the barrel door and withdrew a tile.

He looked up at the audience and said in a quiet voice, "Welcome to this year's Resurrection Bingo." Then he held up the tile and read from it, "G-48".

A quiet, communal holding of breath further stilled the room, as every head dropped to peer at the card on the table in front of it. Here and there a movement as a button was placed on a card. The heads nearby would turn sharply, then quickly back. Now all faces were back toward the speaker.

He had written on a blackboard board behind him. "G-48." He turned the crank again, withdrew another tile, and read it aloud. The scene was repeated as all heads bowed, several buttons were placed, necks craned, then attention returned to the front. The second letter-number combination was written on the board. The crank was turned a third time, a third tile read and recorded, a third episode of frantic concentration.

After the fourth tile was read, the silence was complete. The caller looked over the room. With the "free" space in the middle of the card, the fourth tile was the earliest winning opportunity. I myself had yet to place a single button. Nobody spoke up.

The crank was turned a fifth time, the tile read, the crowd scanned their cards and those of their neighbors. No one spoke up. The caller nodded, then turned the crank. The room had filled with quiet noise. As the remaining tiles were pulled and read, scant attention or concern was paid by those around me, although I was able to place two buttons. When, eight tiles later, someone called out "Bingo", it sounded more like relief than glee.

This was what I had been waiting for. The prize had to be something extraordinary, given the strange draw of the game.

But nothing seemed to happen. Everyone cleared their cards, and the caller erased the board and cranked the handle for the first tile of the next game. I whispered to the woman beside me "No prize?"

"You have to win on the first five calls," she responded without taking her eyes from her card.

"Oh," I said, mostly to myself, although I wasn't sure it made any sense. We played on. The intensity was palpable through the first five calls, then flowed into relief as the game was played out. After about a half-hour of this, I had seen enough. Even though I still didn't understand what was involved, I had miles to drive, and the day wasn't getting any younger. But then I found the first number called in the next game on my card, so figured I'd see one last round through.

I hit on the second one, too. Immediately to the right of the first. "Wouldn't it be a hoot?" I thought. When the third call appeared on my card lined up with the first two, I began to get a little excited. The people to either side of me started to glance at my card nervously. The fourth call was also in the line. Of course, someone could win on four calls if their line passed through the center. But nobody called out.

The crank turned, the tile was read. I checked my card twice, then raised my hand and tentatively called out "Bingo . . . . . ."

The room erupted in noise. People talking out loud, chairs scraping, buttons falling. An attendant hurried over to me and read my marked squares out loud. The caller confirmed each one against the list on the blackboard. "We have a winner," he announced solemnly.

The room went totally, perfectly still. All eyes were on me. The caller spoke across the room, his voice a forced calm.

Francisco Zuniga. *Woman Reposing.* Bronze, 9 x 15 x 7⅞ in., 1966. Collection of The University of Arizona Museum of Art, Tucson. Gift of Dr. and Mrs. Stanley H. Schneider.

"Who do you choose, my son?" he asked. I stared back blankly.

"You must choose now," he urged gently. "I must have a name."

"Uh, choose who?" I stammered, feeling my face flush as all the faces in the room watched me with intense curiosity.

"Your resurrected," he said. When I shrugged, he realized I was clueless and explained, "You can bring one person back from the dead."

I sat frozen in place, my mouth hanging open in stupid wonder. What was he talking about? Of course this could not be true! Back from the dead? Preposterous! Absurd!

But, perhaps it did explain the once-a-year crowd from all over the country, the grim players, the solemn mood.

Then my mind flashed with the hundred horror movies I'd seen. Did they come back as rotting corpses? Did they have the injuries that killed them? If they'd died five hundred years ago, would they be five hundred years old when they came back?

But as the weight of the crowd pressed in on me, and it became clear that I would have to produce a name if just to humor them, I turned my attention to picking the name of a dead person. Maybe this was some sort of test. I got into it. Should I choose some great scientist or leader who could help humanity? A personal friend? Who did I actually know well who had died? As these thoughts reeled through my mind, the man prompted more urgently, "Son, we need your answer now!"

"Karen Sander," I blurted out.

The hall emptied out, and I found myself walking across the muddy lawn toward my car with a frightened woman half my age. She held tightly to my arm and looked about in total confusion. In her 1950s hairstyle and clothing, she looked as out-of-place as I felt.

I walked her around to the passenger side, pressing the car door fob as we went. She slid into the seat, looking even more disoriented as she took in the interior.

"I'll try to explain," I said, as I closed her door. I got into the driver's seat, latched my shoulder strap, and said to her as I started the engine, "Buckle up." She looked at me blankly. I pulled on my shoulder strap as demonstration. Still no comprehension. Finally I leaned over, pulled the buckle across her slender waist and snapped it into place. She looked down at the belt in bewilderment. I had to smile as I pulled out onto the highway and headed north.

We rode in silence. She looked out at the flat Midwestern fields, while I struggled with the reality of her presence and how to explain it to her. She was obviously as profoundly shocked as I was.

"Where are we?" she finally asked.

"Illinois."

She nodded, as though recognizing a place name was a start. Then, just to verify, although a photograph of this very woman had sat in a prominent place in every house I'd lived in for the past fifty years, I asked, "What's your name?"

She looked at me carefully, studying my face as I drove. "Karen," she answered hesitantly. Then more confidently, "Karen Sander."

"Do you know who I am?" I ventured. She hesitated.

"You look a bit like my father. He didn't have a brother, but . . ." she trailed off.

We drove in silence. I didn't know what to say, or even what was real. So I asked, "What year is this?"

She stared ahead, eyes unfocused, pulling up a memory. Her hands, locked together, struggled against each other. Finally, she answered, "It's 1951." Then, as the doubt solidified, "At least, the last I remember." Her face twisted up in anguish, then composed itself. "And, the last thing I remember, I was in Italy with Bill." She paused, then added, "Bill, my husband."

I gripped the wheel. I'd always been socially challenged, so I assumed that whatever I said next would be wrong. So I told her, "You had an accident in Italy. That was fifty years ago. Bill is dead." I made no mention of the fact that he had survived the accident, remarried, and cut me off like a gangrenous limb. I looked over at her as she struggled to make sense of what I'd said.

Then I added, "I'm your son."

She twisted her scarf in her hands, studiously avoiding my eyes. Several miles passed as we each attempted to cope with this new reality. I didn't think she was really seeing the passing landscape, although her pale face was turned to the side window.

But after a few moments she murmured, "It sure is flat around here."

"Yes," I agreed. Just then, we floated up onto an overpass and could see the prairie stretched before us, fading into the distant gray vagueness of the horizon.

"One thing about flat," I said, "you don't have to get very high to be able to see forever."

She nodded, mostly to herself, then drew a ragged breath.

"My son," she said.

"Yes."

"Stephen."

"Yes."

DAVID S. RUBENSTEIN is a painter and writer living in the American Midwest. His art and writing may be viewed at http://www.gruinard.com.

Walking the Sanctuary

No thorns or briers on this trail:
mill pond to woodland to marsh.
Some bird wobbles a song.
I skip the turn for a new trail,

ignore the twinge—
a pebble in my shoe. Here comes

the pond again:
I'm in a loop. A little snake
appears in the path, lifts its head,
tests the world with its tongue.
It's curled all it has.
While I watch, the snake straightens,
reshapes its life.

SHELBY ALLEN takes the long way. She acted in film and theatre, publishes poetry in journals, and organizes poetry programs in Massachusetts prisons. She has learned a lot from the 130-year-old elm trees on her street.

Mother Teresa Would Find It Hard

I AWAKE ON THE BOTTOM OF A THREE-TIER BUNK surrounded by people staring at me. One burly woman asks, "Who are you, and what are you doing here?" I realize I don't fit in, but I must accept the situation, let go of what I want, and find what divine providence has in store for me. I always had enough money, a nice house, and car. Now, surrounded by a ghetto, my home is a bathroom-size, two-woman, cell sunk in a zoo-like dungeon with a sign posted outside the cell: "No Warning Shots Will Be Fired." At first, the only thing to do is sing and drum on the metal desk. A few different tones are possible to make.

I, Shandra Jai, am a songwriter living in a California Women's Facility. It never occurred to me that one day I would be in prison: I've lived a positive, drug-and-alcohol-free, spiritual lifestyle for forty-five out of fifty-five years, but now I am in prison because of a car accident.

A few years ago my brother murdered our mother. At a grand jury trial, I testified against him. I ended up as her heir and became terrified of being next on his list even though he is serving out a life sentence. Performing in the limelight as an artist, I was afraid that he would find someone to hurt me. While shopping, I was convinced someone was following me. I became scared and started drinking alcohol. I got lost in a bad neighborhood looking for a friend's new apartment. All four sides of my car were totaled. Someone said I got out of the car and sat on the curb. I don't remember.

The reality of prison life sinks in, and I decide to make the best of it by using my talents wherever I can. However, at first it seems impossible to encourage women who aren't interested in change. There isn't much rehabilitation in here. In fact, it seems they don't want us to be helped. Mother Teresa would find it hard.

Seven smokers slap dominos on a card table three feet from my head, seven hours a night. I cover my face tightly with the blankets and sheet. If I am around too much tobacco smoke, my throat constricts. How can I remain calm, centered, and compassionate in a world of repressed rage, blame, manipulation, and extreme violence? Very few here take responsibility for their behavior. They dump projections on anyone who will listen. If someone hurts me, I can't tell anyone, or I'll get destroyed for being a snitch. The only way to survive is to stay far within myself, surrendering into a deep level. A month later I am moved to another location. The message: *embrace death and receive life.*

I begin to pay attention to my dreams. I believe our subconscious works through the dream state to alert us to visit new parts of our deeper selves. A Free World staff member sponsors a Dream Group. I notice that I am afraid of angry, ignorant people and fear their power to hurt me. I wonder if I am here to learn how to deal with this fear.

One day I am sitting by the door of a dayroom full of 256 women on torn, black couches with foam easing out. It's "good to be bad." No sign of anything else. Out of nowhere an inmate kneels down to comfort me, saying, "You never know when you might meet an angel." I look into her eyes experiencing her as an angel and write:

Like a mirror in the angel's heart
Her love shines bright as the brightest star.
Like a candle burnin' in the dark
Her smile brings life to those who haven't come this far.

Songs begin to emerge with no instrument to play. Pencils and paper are hard to find, so I clap my hands, sing in the shower to set the tone, invent a primitive way to jot it all down. Soon I have written ten songs. The only quiet place to be is outside, sitting on the ground. This becomes my composing space. Eventually, I have a battery-operated keyboard, headphones, and CD player on which I play ocean sounds. The most difficult part is finding a space inside my head to compose. Constant noise is everywhere. It's popular to scream and cry out; there is so much suffering here. In the summer it can be well over a hundred degrees. I pretend I'm inside a giant sauna, cleansing the toxins from my body. I listen to the sound of the ocean or a stream on the CD player to block noise. Rarely do I talk to

Opposite:
Bernice Cross.
Stone Angel.
Oil and sand on canvas,
24 x 14$\frac{1}{8}$ in., 1950.
The Phillips Collection,
Washington, D.C.
Acquired 1950.

anyone, and I don't take complaints. After two years, I complete the lyrics and music for forty new songs.

I'm not Catholic, but it is quiet and cooler in the church. After several months, the heat gets to me, so I devise a working schedule of writing lyrics and music during the week and on the weekends switch to hard oak chairs and meditate with humility. For one year I practice patience, silence, and listening. During one meditation, I hear, *Carve your niche.* Faith is needed since there are so many rules and limitations, and this place is a storage house for punishment.

The chaplain, a nun who used to be a professional tennis player, has a wonderful, nonstop sense of humor. I find myself going just to see her. She is from the "old traditional school of thought" and wears the traditional nun's uniform with head covering. If she had a whip, she'd crack it, but not in a mean way, just to make a point. She cracks you up with her humor. She has a photo hanging on the door of herself with the Pope. She likes to repeat her story of meeting the Pope.

Months later, I ask the chaplain if I can sing on my birthday. This debut opens up a sincere connection between us. She pulls me outside, away from the others, to delve into the unknown and discuss life's deeper mysteries. I love being with her! Our eyes are exactly the same size, shape, and color. Eventually she comes down with Parkinson's and must retire. I write a funny song and ask her to sit in front of me in church as I perform in front of a full house:

Song to Sister Kathleen

You walked the way that Mary paved
With a heart of compassion, sincerely gave.
When Jesus died, his children were saved.
You came here to serve and chose to stay.

You could be playin' tennis, or married to the Pope.
Bought a house in Jamaica, smoke a lotta dope.
Met a wealthy doctor, had children all your own.
Baked a thousand and one cookies, talkin' all day on the phone.

Instead, you're spendin' precious time with us.
We're women in need who need your loving touch.
Renew our strength, faith, hope and trust.
Enlighten us, undo all the fuss.

You say there's no precious time to waste.
We're women in need who need your smiling face.
We come into your safe and peaceful space
Enlighten us with humor, heal crime in every race.

The chaplain gives me permission to do my own concert for Christmas. The women are touched. After she retires, a new sister takes her place. She is liberal and open-minded and allows me on holidays to teach a series of Expressive Arts workshops in the sanctuary. My workshops are for inmates to get in touch with their better selves in a safe space where they can express their uniqueness.

During a workshop, the sanctuary is complete with watercolors, crayons, chalk, colored pencils, markers, glitter, sponge shapes, and brushes ready to roll. The doors open and sixty or more women crowd in. The day is spent doing sacred movement, fun improvisation games to loosen up, and writing poems and stories, which are painted and shared in front of the group. Laughter circles the church. I say, "We're going to the island of . . ." And someone says, "Christian." I continue, "And on the island there are . . ." "Little Shroud of Turin hats made of twigs and branches," completes my sentence. It is amazing to see all the beautiful creations. Everyone yearns for peace, love, Jesus, happiness, friendship, joy, and connection. The workshops grow in popularity. Soon so many people sign up, we have to turn some away. I play my keyboard and sing my own songs. I give the microphone to anyone else who wants to sing.

Some can't read, spell, or speak English. I walk around encouraging them to explore new territory. A woman in a wheelchair, confused about what to write about her deceased mother, has a breakthrough as she gets in touch with her emotions. I roll her over to the art table. Another inmate wears a helmet for seizures. She enjoys smearing her hands in paint and stamping them on her friend's shirt. I write:

Welcome to the resting place,
A place for rebels, sinners, and saints.
Lay your head, make your bed,
Inside a world away from what was said.

To experience their transformations is rewarding. I look into other souls and see joy, where just a minute ago there was no hope. Everyone lines up to use the microphone and present her final piece. Some share dreams for family members, the desire to be closer to God, a personal insight, or an appreciation. What! They actually listened to my opening speech about honestly expressing where they are? We hang their creations around the church and outside in the glass case.

One day a stranger comes up to me and says, "Aren't you a songwriter? There are auditions tonight in the band room." That night, I wait impatiently in a tiny end room. A few inmates sing a capella, others try playing the guitar. Memory and pressure make it difficult for me to remember any songs, so I make something up on the spot.

The next day the drummer comes up to me and says, "I need you in the band!" Secretly, I know she is in charge of picking the women because she played professionally for Joan Jett in the seventies. She and the bass player have the skill and experience to create a strong foundation. I am chosen to be the keyboard player. The bass player, tall with platinum hair, is a Christian country-rock professional. The lead singer sounds like Janis Joplin. The flute player, who has been here for a long time, can play anything. Our band's name is "Just Us Blues." Our state-issue clothes are blue, and we all want justice.

Being aware that I am a support player, not the star, I work on a different set of skills: concentration, confidence, keeping in rhythm with the group, and memorization. I keep my ego out of the way and learn their songs in service of a bigger picture. I sing a few of my own songs, learn twenty others, and master the intention to play each song without making mistakes. Out of 4,000 women, it is a privilege to have been chosen.

The summer brings together an outdoor concert, and we sound great. Everyone has such a good time they forget they are in here. We perform a mixture of rock with some Christian songs. Songs like: "Can You Imagine," "House of the Rising Sun," "Dreams" (Fleetwood Mac), "Summertime," "Moondance," and "Piece of My Heart" (Joplin). The concert is a breakthrough for the prison. *Mother Teresa would be in the front row dancing!*

I am an emotionally stable human being. I am not a person to fear. I made a mistake, and I am paying for it. It is an awful situation, but I am making the best of it. Thanks for listening and sorry for my mistakes. I love not being perfect. It really makes me happy, the one element I never experienced before. Money and comfort are superficial. I am happy to own nothing and to be without money, to experience the connection within myself and God at the deepest levels. What a blessing. I pray that I will stand the ground and hold spirit close in my heart, no matter what.

An adopted child, SHANDRA JAI's parents introduced her to classical and popular piano music at age seven. She started writing songs in third grade on a black and red twenty-five-dollar guitar. In college, she began an inward journey to find her "true self." "I was eating with Hare Krishnas, meditating with Buddhists, dancing with Sufis, singing with Unity Churches, listening to Ram Das, and chanting with Tibetans until I settled within." Musically gifted, Shandra has been performing original songs since 1976. She found her biological brothers and sisters in 1984. One sister is an oboe player. Her great-grandparents were concert pianists. Shandra has four CDs to her credit. You can listen to her music at www.cdbaby.com.

CAROL HAMILTON

Three Kings Day

Día de Los Tres Reyes Magos

All of the bakery windows
are full of sweet bread rings
with a pink plastic Baby Jesus
hidden within. A sleek limousine stops,
and great piles of wreath-sized rings
are carried out on a strong man's shoulder,
are slipped inside, driven off to a party.
The Indian mothers, each with her quiet
tread and downcast eyes, pass holding a child
by one hand and a bag of pastries
in the other. We buy two
the size of a woman's palm. The churches
and the bakeries are full and alight,
and the plaza. Who can stay away
as we remind one another that
we are warm-skinned and breathing,
still we are miracles here. Young children
wear velvet capes and crowns
covered with gold or silver paper.
The kings are wandering, searching
tonight. Their eyes are star struck.
And a child is hidden away.
There is every reason to expect
that we shall find him once dawn
and our hunger return to us.
But for this night, we are expectant,

milling around in a lighted darkness,
buying and selling our hopes,
carrying them home in frail
boxes and paper bags.

CAROL HAMILTON has recent and upcoming work in *Atlanta Review, Nimrod, Bogg, Karamu, Blue Unicorn, The Arorean, Willow Review, Mad Poet's Review, Freefall, Southwestern American Literature, Distillery, Phoebe, Cider Press Review, Re:Al,* and *Abbey.* She is a former poet laureate of Oklahoma and has been nominated for a Pushcart Prize five times. Her twelfth book, a new poetry chapbook, *Shots On,* is from Finishing Line Press (May 2008). She is a former elementary teacher, college and university professor, and currently translates at a clinic for women and children.

New Racket

When I was a kid, I used to pray every night for a new bicycle. Then I realized that the Lord doesn't work that way, so I stole one and asked for forgiveness.

—EMO PHILIPS (1956–)

Leah C. Olivier.
Racket and Ball.
Pen and ink, 1991.

WHEN I NODDED OFF WHILE DRIVING my Ford Ranger pickup and ran down an embankment on a back road in Vermont two summers ago, smacking a two-hundred-year-old oak tree, I reached to turn off the ignition and saw my right hand dangling uselessly. Looking back, I realize my first, untutored response was relief.

Not so much because I had broken my wrist and not my head, but because it meant I likely would never play tennis again.

For sixty years tennis has been the mostly unwelcome measure of my worth.

When I was six or seven years old, my mother inaugurated my love-hate relationship with the game on a red clay tennis court in Charlotte. She would hit with me for hours—"Come on, Mom, give me another lob"—until I was eleven or twelve when she had debilitating colon surgery. We had moved to the Philippines by then, and my tennis future was passed on to my fiercely competitive father. I have never been sure whether he had the huge ambitions for my tennis career I felt from him or if I have made him the bearer of my own dashed hopes.

The summer I turned fifteen we were on leave back in Charlotte. In a team match, I played against the boy who had just won the Charlotte sixteen-and-under city tournament. His coach, Dick McKee, the University of Miami coach, had nurtured me through my early years in the game.

I beat him in three sets. Dick told me afterwards he thought I was the strongest fifteen-year-old in the mid-south. Later that summer I took a set off my father for the first terrifying time. I believed I was on my way to stardom . . . and a niche in the elusive Hall of Self-esteem.

In high school I played all four years, winning most of my matches. The summer I would turn eighteen my doubles partner and I entered a regional tournament in Chattanooga. Being unknown, we drew the Mexican Davis Cup doubles team in the first round. They had just arrived on the plane from Mexico City, were jet-lagged and unused to the heavy, low-altitude Tennessee air. We won the first three games without losing a point.

It was to be as high as I would climb in tennis. We lost the next twelve games. In the consolation round, we met a team our own age from California who shamed us with their high level of play.

I played for a year in college, then turned to carousing, telling myself it was a better choice. For several years after college, I vegged, playing occasionally, just enough to wake those synapses that triggered disappointment with every overhead dumped into the net.

At around age thirty I began playing again. Although I loved the strenuous exercise, my chronic disappointment at my game, having arrested at sixteen, was still torment. I embarrassed myself with my bad temper when I hit poor shots.

I have been a fairly active player since then, trying to persuade myself not so much that my game is wonderful, as I once hoped it might be, but that running around a tennis court at sixty-five should be reward enough. And sometimes it was. But often, as I went deep into the backhand court and took a mighty swing to pass my opponent crosscourt, the pitiful result would provoke painful memories of past near-glory.

The chief remnant from my sixteen-year-old game was unbecoming adolescent pique.

After my accident, I asked the young orthopedic surgeon—who had masterfully reconstructed my shattered wrist—whether I would ever play tennis again. She had no way of knowing what a loaded question it was.

"That's going to be our goal," she replied noncommittally.

Six months of physical therapy and using my left hand, I finally could tie my shoes and pull a T-shirt over my head. One day I snuck my racket out of the closet, went into the garage, and tried hitting a ball against the wall. Didn't work.

A month later I asked my wife, Lacey, if she would try hitting gently in the short court with me. It was awkward, but I could do it.

And I loved it!

For the next couple of weeks, I hit balls against the bang board. Then Lacey hit full court with me. A couple of weeks later, I screwed up my courage and asked a friend if he would hit with me. We played for an exhilarating hour. My strength was pitiful, but just hitting the ball at all was a thrill. I stopped only because the odd way I gripped the racket raised a blister on my hand that began to bleed before I noticed it.

A year later I still can't grip the racket quite right, and there are a few basic shots I simply no longer have. I often take a hard swing and only get the ball back to mid-court.

Oddly, my poor manners still emerge when I lose a point I think I should have won. My aging opponents think I am the same old guy they have played against for years. How could they know that even the swearing at missed shots is fun now?

Three or four times a week on the drive to Brattleboro, I pass that old oak tree in my new truck. Aside from some bumper-high bark missing, she looks fine, as if she will go on for another century or so. I like to think my mother—who has been dead twenty-four years— borrowed a piece of that old tree to help me regain, no, at long last, *to receive* the pleasure of the game she introduced to me sixty years ago.

As I pass the tree, I blow her a kiss.

BLAYNEY COLMORE was an Episcopal parish priest for thirty years. His vision of a creation in which our species is subject to serendipity created consternation and delight among parishioners and continues to feed his curiosity about the purpose of ego in the ongoing evolution of the cosmos. Blayney sends, to those interested—and to some who likely are not—periodic e-mails, "Notes from Zone 10" (California) and "Notes from Zone 4" (Vermont). *In the Zone: Notes on Wondering Coast to Coast* (2002) and *God Knows: It's Not About Us* (2006) are available from Xlibris and major outlets.

Burning Both Ends

This heart of mine is no wax stick,
but see the flames upon it?
Love has lit the wick wound through my body
and into this late night of you having had fever,
now sleeping and the peepers calling and calling
so many hot songs.
Restless rain is falling on your rooftop
but it extinguishes nothing.
This house that I'm in, yours, and my own flesh,
my open eyes can just barely contain my luminescence.
Daylight breaks.
The woodpecker hammers your tin chimney,
attracting a mate. I leave a note,
wander down wet roads toward home,
fog lifting off of warming hillsides,
buds bursting into green,
every tree a candle to the low sun.
A robin with burning chest,
arsonist,
alights here and there,
yearning for worms and singing
about what beauty will remain
after all this combustion
and hunger
has its way.

ASHER PUCCIARELLO is a child and family therapist and a writer. He decreased work on his second novel as he awaited the birth of his first child, who is now in the world. There is something stunning, he says, about waiting and then witnessing the arrival. Words seem extraneous.

Tom Thumb at Chambersburg

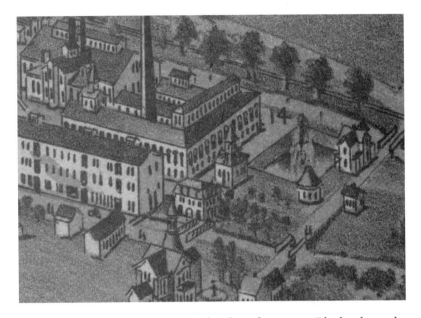

Chambursburg,
Pennsylvania, 1894.

TOWARD THE END OF JULY, on the last leg of our tour, Bleeker brought us up into Pennsylvania. We were three nights in Pittsburgh, then briefly in McKeesport, Donegal, and Manns Choice. And then, on a warm Friday afternoon, we arrived in Chambersburg and made our way to the Franklin Hotel.

It was a pleasant little town with handsome buildings, many with fancy façades and stone columns, and rows of stores along Main Street with colorful awnings.

Before the battle of Gettysburg, Robert E. Lee had camped his army in the neighboring fields and hills, a sprawling corps of more than sixty thousand. The hotel owner, a stout, black-haired man with an egg-shaped growth on his forehead, told us what a mess it had been having all those soldiers around. "You never know what's on the way," the proprietor said, sounding as if he was looking forward to the next bit of excitement. He was proud of his town and proud of its long history, and he urged us to stop in the cemetery before we left, for a look at the old headstones. And I, after a day's travel, was thinking sure, why not, just what I need, an old graveyard.

We performed that evening in the Masonic Hall, and were scheduled to appear again the following afternoon—Vinny and I, with her sister Minnie, and Commodore Nutt, billed as *Barnum's Quartet of Dwarfs*—doing our songs and dances, and a few jokes and impersonations, our usual fare.

After the evening performance, we returned to our hotel rooms exhausted, except for Kellogg and Richardson and Harry Nobbs, who lingered at the bar. When Vinny and I reached our room, Vinny turned to me with a slow, needful look and said what she would really like, at that moment, was a macaroon.

I winced. "In this town? You think they have macaroons?"

"Char-lie," she said, pleading.

"But nothing's open."

"Up the block," she said. "I saw a place. We passed it just now, coming back from the hall."

I went down into the night, small me, thirty-six inches tall, Charlie Stratton, known to the world as Tom Thumb. Looking around, I spotted a shop with its lamps still lit. They sold crackers, bread, walnuts, and incidentals. The girl behind the counter was mesmerized by my smallness, couldn't take her eyes off me. She had no idea what a macaroon might be.

"We have lemon drops," she said.

"Nothing else?"

"Chocolate pound cake, but it's stale."

I bought the lemon drops.

Back at the room, Vinny's face sagged with disappointment. "I can't eat these," she said. "They'll ruin my teeth."

I took one, and, as lemon drops go, it wasn't half bad.

"They had some beef jerky. You would have liked some of that?"

"Don't be silly," she said.

She took a lemon drop and put it in her mouth. "They could have put more lemon in it," she said.

I took another, and she took another, and we did that for a while, sitting on the bed, crunching lemon drops, she in her nightshift and I in my street clothes. And before long, fatigue set in. She leaned back upon her pillow, and, faster than I knew, she was swallowed up in sleep. And the same with me, soon after. So tired, I just passed out, in my shirt and pants.

I don't recall that I had any dreams that night, though I know there are people—Barnum is one—who say we always dream, and when we seem not to, it's because the dream was too deeply buried to be remembered. In any case, I was wrenched awake by the sound of a big gun firing. Vinny too—yanked out of sleep. And no doubt everyone in town.

It was half past three in the morning, and when I went to the window, a thin slice of the moon was up and the sky was full of stars. And again the sound of that gun. I stepped into the corridor, and Minnie and the Commodore came out of their rooms, and some of the others, in nightshifts. Bleeker was up and dressed already—or, like me, had never changed out of his day clothes. He went down to see what he could learn.

Moments later he was back, saying a Confederate force had arrived in the night and was bivouacked on the hills west of town. The firing was from a gun that General Crouch's men had set up on the Pittsburgh Pike, to hold them off. But it was hopeless. All he had was fifty men. The regiments that had been based in the town had been siphoned off to bolster the defenses around Washington.

"Pack your things," he told everybody. "Better to be ready."

I went back to the room, and while Vinny dressed, I stashed our things into the luggage. Through the window I saw wagons and buckboards pulling up to the stores along the street and lights coming on—shopkeepers rushing in and pulling merchandise out of their stores, riding off with as much as they could. At the bank there were two coaches and five or six guards with rifles, the bank people filling the coaches with sacks of money.

Vinny left to help her sister, and I found Bleeker in his room, buckling up his bags. His wife, Julia, had gone to help the Commodore.

"What do you think?" I asked.

"I don't know," he answered.

His mind was racing. So was mine.

We went down to the lobby, and the others followed. The lobby crowded up, and the night clerk was telling people there was a room in the cellar where they could store their luggage and valuables. And we knew what he was saying—that the Rebs would grab anything they could carry.

Ben Kellogg had the box with the jewelry and the cash receipts. He never went anywhere without it. Under his long jacket, he carried a pistol on his hip. "I think I'll just keep the box with me," he said.

Bleeker was busy thinking, eyes darting, intense, fierce. And suddenly he was all decision.

"I need a wagon and a coach," he said, stepping over to the night clerk, a slim, dull-eyed fellow with sideburns, thirtyish, in black pants, a blue vest over his white shirt. His necktie was a black shoelace tied in a bow.

"Impossible," he answered. "You see how it is. The ones with wagons, they're carting their valuables into the hills. It's routine, whenever the rebs come near."

Bleeker took out a roll of bills, peeled off two fifties, and stuffed them into the fellow's vest pocket. And that did it. "I'll see what I can do," he said.

He darted out of the lobby, and while he was gone, we were out front, on the portico, waiting. When he returned, he pulled up with a wagon drawn by a scraggly horse.

"That the best you can find?" Bleeker said, unhappy with the horse.

"Beggars can't be choosers," the clerk said. He had thin lips with an odd curl at the corners that seemed almost a sneer. "And you better just forget about getting that coach you were hopin' for."

"Then find another wagon."

"Already paid everything you give me for this one and offered my solemn promise you would bring it back," he said. "I don't think you appreciate the big favor I just done you."

Bleeker stared at the clerk, and I could see that he didn't trust him. Nor did I. Still, he took out two more fifties and offered them.

"I'll be back," the fellow said, with a slick nod, grabbing the cash, and, on foot, he disappeared up the street. The sky was brightening, the faintest glimmer of dawn.

*P. T. Barnum
and General Tom Thumb.*
At age five, Charles Sherwood Stratton (1838–1883) was close to the same height as when he was six months old (25 inches). P. T. Barnum, a distant relative of Stratton's family, became interested in the small boy. Barnum taught Stratton how to perform and gave him the stage name of Tom Thumb. At the age of five, Stratton made his first tour of America with Barnum, eventually becoming an international celebrity. At age nine, he began to grow slowly, reaching 3 feet, 4 inches high by the time of his death at the age of forty-five.

Bleeker told the luggage boys to fetch the trunks and baggage from the rooms and to load them onto the wagon. He sent Sam, the groom, to get the ponies and the dwarf coach from the stable. He told Kellogg to stay by the wagon and guard it with his life.

We went inside to check on the women, and they were already on their way down. The Commodore was fidgety, asking when and where to pick up some breakfast.

Julia rummaged in her carryall and came up with a muffin wrapped in a napkin from last night's dinner and offered it to the Commodore. He took it and stepped away, not wanting us to watch as he ate it.

We waited on the portico for the night clerk. The boys had all the luggage aboard the wagon, with the dwarf carriage lashed down on top and the ponies tethered to the rear.

The night clerk wasn't back yet. "I gave him too much," Bleeker said. "He never spent a damn nickel for that nag and the wagon. Stole it from some back alley and took what else I gave him and got his ass out of here."

But still we waited.

Then the hotel proprietor rode up on a black mare.

"Looks bad," he said.

"How bad?" Bleeker asked.

"They'll for sure sack the town and do damage. Bastard rebs are hungry, and they forage for what they can get. Better for you to get out while you can."

"That's what we're trying to do," Bleeker said.

It was going on half past five, and just then three cannon shots were fired into the town, one ball smashing into a shop just up the street. The proprietor rushed off, riding fast, and Bleeker, like a man possessed, swiftly sent the two baggage boys off with the wagon, pointing them to the road that would take them to Fayetteville and then on to Gettysburg. "We'll catch up with you there," he said, and sent the groom with them, and Richardson too, the pianist, since there was room for one more. He kept Kellogg and the jewelry box with us.

We were braced for more cannon fire, but there was none. Moments after the wagon disappeared from view, a heap of Confederate cavalry came thundering in, arriving on many different streets from different directions, and foot soldiers, too, appearing to our left and right.

"Inside, inside," Bleeker shouted, herding us back into the lobby.

Then we waited, and it seemed forever. A few officers appeared on the portico, talking animatedly. Then more officers. One, grim-faced, stepped inside, glanced about at the mob, and stepped back out.

Stratton married Lavinia Warren in 1863 at Grace Episcopal Church in New York City followed by a reception for 2,000 guests. The wedding made the front-page of newspapers across the world. The best man (far left) was George Washington Morrison ("Commodore Nutt"), who also performed with Barnum. The maid of honor was Minnie Warren, Lavinia's sister. The newlyweds were received by President Lincoln at the White House after the wedding.

Julia took a bag of peanuts out of her mesh carryall and passed them around, and we sat there, cracking open the soft shells and crunching on the nuts. A woman was humming to her baby. A tall man blew his nose. A bearded man paced by the door.

When the proprietor returned, he was puffy-faced and swollen, the anger inside him simmering. He stood by the desk and in a strong, tense voice told what he knew.

The officer in charge, he said, was General McCausland, with orders from Jubal Early to collect a tribute from the town or burn it to the ground. "They want a hundred thousand in gold coin or half a million in Union currency."

A low moan limped through the lobby.

"Will they pay it?" the man with the beard called out.

The manager rubbed his hands together and swung his head from side to side, as if struggling to avoid the bad news he was here to give us. "It doesn't seem likely or even possible," he said, and again the low, restless moan, folding and unfolding. "The town elders say there ain't near enough cash in the town, which is true. The bank moved its reserves up to Harrisburg soon as they learned of the troops on the hill. Right now the parties are still talking, but frankly folks, it don't look good. People in town are gathering what they can and going off to the fields and hills. And I would urge all of you to do the same."

He warned us that looting had already begun. They were breaking into homes and shops and taking whiskey and whatever caught their fancy. Some were already drunk. He told us to stay in groups because it was getting wild out there, soldiers grabbing hats and purses, pulling rings off fingers. He told the women to hide their jewelry.

"Why?" someone called out, the woman with the baby. "Why are they doing this awful thing?"

"For compensation, that's what they say."

"For what?"

Again he swung his head from side to side, with obvious discomfort. "Well, it's tit for tat, you see. General Hunter, right or wrong, burned a bunch of houses in the valley, in the Shenandoah. The local farmers were killing his men in the night, and the big landowners and the governor were encouraging it. So Hunter torched some big houses in the vicinity of the murders. A few of those houses belonged to folks with close ties to Jeff Davis."

The proprietor stepped over and told Bleeker to swaddle us in towels and carry us out as if we were babies. "Some of them out there are crazy drunk—you want nothing that will catch their attention. If they see the dwarfs, they'll be on you for sure."

Bleeker held Vinny in one arm and me in the other, and, many steps behind us, Harry Nobbs carried Minnie and the Commodore, each of us wrapped in a blue towel the proprietor had found for us, only our faces showing.

A soldier stopped Bleeker, a bottle of whiskey in one hand, a pistol in the other, wanting to know what Bleeker was carrying. When he saw our faces, Vinny's and mine, he laughed and stepped away. "Two of 'em huh? Been keepin' your woman busy, I see. Where is she? She got another in the oven?"

While the soldier was talking, Harry Nobbs went right past and waited for us up ahead. Then on we went, all of us, with Julia and the wardrobe woman, Mabel, and Kellogg with the cash box. We saw soldiers kicking doors in, entering houses and breaking up the furniture, creating piles of splintered wood ready to be torched.

Some though, I saw, were unhappy with the goings-on, and they were helping the families in whatever ways they could. One lugged an old woman's sewing machine to a safe spot away from the houses. Two soldiers carried a corpse out of a house where it was being waked and buried it in a shallow grave in the garden, so the fire wouldn't get to it. But many were looting, coming out of houses with things they'd taken—a fancy pillow, a copper kettle, a bearskin rug, a crystal chandelier. One wore a calico dress over his uniform, with a cigar in his mouth, his carbine in one hand and a bottle of rum in the other.

We turned a corner, and I saw a soldier knock a man down and take the satchel he was carrying, but it held nothing, only some clothes, and he pulled them out and threw them around on the street. Farther along, a woman was screaming and wailing in front of her house—a soldier slapped her in the face and shoved her to the ground. "Keep movin', keep movin'," a sergeant shouted at Bleeker, and soon we were out of it, away from the grid of streets, the brick buildings and wooden houses, and Bleeker carried us up a hill and into a cemetery, where many of the townspeople were gathering.

General McCausland had the main body of his force on the fairgrounds by the Pittsburgh Pike. I saw them out there, in the morning light, about a mile or two off. And, all around us, people talking, murmuring, coughing, sobbing. Somebody said it was about two thousand troops out there, on the fairgrounds.

We sat on the grass, on somebody's grave, looking down at the town. Vinny leaned against me, my arm around her waist, and Minnie leaned against her. The Commodore sat a few feet away, huddled, clutching himself, his back against a gravestone.

People were scattered across the hill and neighboring fields, standing, sitting, holding each other, some just arriving out of the town, with satchels, blankets, and baggage filled with any of the little things they'd been able to rescue. The sun was low and rising, the air warm, no clouds, a few horses wandering free. From where we were, we saw right down into the town—the houses, shops, livery stables, the square brick bank close by the Franklin Hotel. The courthouse with its tall columns. The streets at right angles to each other, dividing the town into large square blocks, like a quilt blanket, with low trees along some of the streets, and McCausland's soldiers running about and doing their worst. Dogs and goats loose on the streets, and pigs. Chickens out of their coops.

Suddenly a massive flash of flame from the town hall, and smoke rising. Then flame exploding through the open windows of the courthouse, and then a warehouse, and houses and shops all around, to the east and west of Main Street, soldiers at key points lighting the fires simultaneously. Long black columns of smoke rose in the morning sky, hundreds of them, weaving and snaking about. The air filled with the hissing and crackling of flames and with the woeful moaning of animals trapped and dying. How fast and sudden it was, win-

Chambersburg, Pennsylvania, located about twenty miles north of the Mason-Dixon line, was always in close proximity to the war. In 1864, Brigadier General John McCausland and his two cavalry brigades reached Chambersburg about 3 AM on July 30, where they joined Colonel William Peters and his 21st Virginia Cavalry. A year after the Battle of Gettysburg, the Confederacy was close to defeat. Chambersburg was to become the place for retaliation. Lieutenant General Jubal Anderson Early of the Confederate Army ordered McCausland to march into Chambersburg, demand $100,000 in gold or $500,000 in greenbacks as compensation for houses that General Hunter's Union troops had burned in Virginia. Union soldiers tried to hold off the Confederates, but they were greatly outnumbered.

dows bursting and rifle cartridges in cabinets and bottom drawers exploding, and the roar of roofs and brick walls collapsing. And then the many columns of smoke bending, coming together into a single huge column, black and dense, and, at the very top, the column flattened and spread out weirdly, in a mushroom shape, blocking the sun and bringing on an eerie darkness.

The thick stem of the mushroom turning now like a twister, sucking things up from below—bedsheets, burning shingles, sheets of newspaper, anything loose that it touched, pieces of clothing, lifting things then letting them fall away. And the sound of it, a hum, a buzz, a hiss, and the stink catching at the back of my throat, smell of tar and wood burning, leather, cardboard, silk. It hovered over the town square, and then it roved east along Market Street, a swirling funnel of smoke and flame. It seemed, somehow, the end of the world, and that's what it was for the people on the hill. The town was gone; they had lost everything.

Then I was aware that I was standing, but couldn't remember getting up. Vinny was still on the grass, holding Minnie, both arms around her, and Minnie looking away from the fire, her head on Vinny's shoulder. Vinny was stroking her back. The Commodore was where he'd been, crouched against a gravestone. There was a boulder nearby, and I went to it and climbed up for a better look. The funnel was dissipating, but the houses and buildings still burned, and, high above the town, the cloud of smoke and haze lingered, and the sky remained dark.

All that was left of the bank was part of a stone wall and the four columns that had supported the portico. And much the same with the courthouse, the columns remaining, rising amid the scattered bricks and stones from the walls that had fallen, smoke wafting from the smoldering interior. Where the homes and shops had stood, brick chimneys rose like long, blackened fingers. As I scanned the streets and avenues, it seemed about two-thirds of the town had burned, homes, shops, stables, sheds, the hall where we had performed last evening and were to perform today. It was worst in the downtown area, by the bank and the courthouse, the destruction spreading over some ten square blocks. The hotel where we slept and the restaurant

Bank of Chambersburg
after the town's burning.

across the street where we had eaten. And the shop where I had bought lemon drops for Vinny.

It was eleven o'clock, and only then did I notice that the hill to the west was deserted. McCausland and his cavalry had pulled out. A few soldiers were still in the town, stragglers, or rear guard, some moving down Market Street, inspecting the ruins, others darting about, in and out of the homes that had escaped damage, taking whatever they could carry.

People began to move off the hill, back into town, for a closer look at the devastation. And us, we too were up, but not moving, just standing, looking. "I hate all this," Vinny said. "I hate it. Hate it." She was weeping. Minnie, facing the town now, was frozen, as in a trance, the knuckle of one of her fingers anchored in her mouth.

The Commodore was also up, gazing at the ruins, seeming dazed and confused, and frightened. "I want to go home," he said, looking down into the smoldering town, and when he said that, I realized that I didn't know where home was for him. I knew he was from New Hampshire, but from a village or a city, in the mountains or by the ocean, I had no idea.

"Take me home, please," he said, to no one in particular, sounding not at all like himself. His eyes were still fastened on the ruins, and he was motionless, gazing like a child who was lost and didn't know where he was.

NICHOLAS RINALDI offers courses in literature and creative writing at Fairfield University in Connecticut. His poems and short stories have appeared widely. Three of his novels and three collections of his poetry have been published. His most recent novel is *Between Two Rivers* (Harper-Collins, New York, and Bantam, London). The present story is part of a work-in-progress, a work of historical fiction. Tom Thumb, in fact, was not present at the burning of Chambersburg. The event was real, however, and the details about the burning and about the behavior of the soldiers have been taken from eyewitness accounts.

Emergence

This spring
the rhododendron stands tall
in her great cobalt pot.

Last year she bore
her one blossom bravely,
while the bougainvillea
shimmered with a thousand
easy petals, and the princess tree
strutted her purple robes.

No amount of coaxing
could draw her forth.

This year that rhododendron
has preempted the season.
Her arms burst with vermillion
bells. Hummingbirds
are dazzled, refusing to leave
her side.

She teaches trust
in the hidden
ways of creation,

belief in the moment
of emergence—exquisite,
never to be hurried.

KATHRYN RIDALL is a poet and transpersonally oriented psychotherapist in the San Francisco Bay Area. Her poems have appeared in dozens of journals such as *Kalliope* and *Pearl*. Several poems have been finalists in contests. She recently won two 2007 Maggi H. Meyer Poetry Awards.

JOSEPH B. HEIMER

Shadows of the Phoenix

The Duality of Renewal and Change

APRIL 1919 WAS A SAD MONTH. The great convulsions of fire and death ravaging mankind had abated. The Great War, which we would later call World War I, was finally over. Nine million human beings had perished, an incalculably greater number crippled in mind or body. Nations lay in ruins, bodies in heaps. Many were those who said, "this must never happen again!" Twenty years later, it would not only happen again but take an even more terrible form. Hitler, Stalin, the Holocaust, and Hiroshima—all these waited malevolently in the future. But no one knew that in 1919. At that time, most felt relieved it had at last ended.

Around the world, people tried to pick up the pieces and go back to their previous lives, but for many there was no going back. The war had changed everything, and most especially it had changed those who fought it. Now, in the first spring following the Armistice, some men journeyed to the places where they had killed and others died, often not for any reason they could express. Today we would call it a desire for "closure," but for these mostly unschooled, simple yet now cynical men, it took the form of a vague, undefined longing.

Here, in eastern France, the battlefield of Verdun lay still and quiet beneath the mild spring sunshine. In a vicious, ten-month ordeal, 600,000 men had been gassed, blown up, or shot—far too many to ever bury, even had many of them not already been blown into fragments. The struggle had devoured men like a gluttonous beast and stripped away all trees, animals, grass, and nearly all signs of human

73

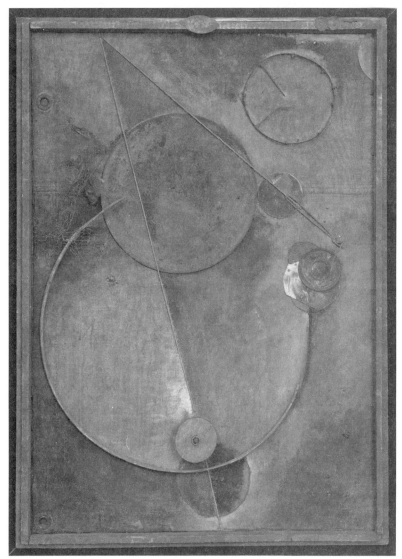

habitation. Nothing remained but cratered dirt, crumbling trenches, shattered military equipment, and, above all, corpses to mark the place where an entire generation's lifeblood had been poured out.

But the ex-soldiers standing around now, slack-jawed and unable to speak, could hardly believe their eyes. Here in hell's anteroom, where high-explosives had sundered man and earth alike, they now saw saplings, grass, and birds chirping noisily in the morning breeze. Surely, they thought, this could not be the same place. Surely the pain and horror could not vanish so easily. And yet they had. Nature, with her customary sublime indifference to men's quarrels, had gone on with her cycle of rebirth and renewal. To many, it seemed almost obscene. To others, it almost looked as if nature tried to forget, just as mankind was trying to forget, the horror of the previous four years.

The natural world had begun the slow but inexorable process of renewal. The scars on the minds and souls of these veterans, however, would take much longer to heal and and would never fade away entirely. Still, superficially at least, the world was recovering. Nations were rebuilding, culture was flowing, and economies were rebounding. Musicians were playing music again instead of firing machine guns; scientists were inventing things for making life better rather than destroying it. Many used the word "renewal" to describe all this, but it was a renewal borne of fire.

Classical imagery portrays the phoenix as a bird of fire which rises from its own ashes after consuming itself, in a perpetual cycle of death and rebirth. In the natural world, death and decay in various forms do the same thing by providing nutrients to developing life. It requires no great leap of imagination to draw analogies between these concepts and the process of renewal in our own lives. Unlike the phoenix, however, we are not mythological; and unlike the natural world of plants, animals, and insects we are not merely creatures of biology. Humans are indeed organisms in the concrete, biological sense, but we are also God's unique creation in His own image. We are both physical and spiritual, and the two interact in ways we cannot fully comprehend. Any understanding of renewal must acknowledge that it is a unique duality between change and the individual, both physically and spiritually.

HOW DOES AN INDIVIDUAL EXPERIENCE SPIRITUAL RENEWAL?
Renewal means "to be made new again," and yet "newness" implies something that was not there before. Conversely, "again" indicates a return to an earlier state of affairs. Because human existence has a spiritual as well as a physical component, we experience renewal through the dynamics of their interactions. The key is change.

With nature, renewal follows an identifiable pattern in the seasons and in the reproductive patterns of organisms. While humans conform to this natural process of change in strictly biological terms, humans also impose their own will upon the process. A man who willingly goes without food in order to feed someone else is doing precisely that—he is introducing change to the body through his spirit. If he finds this selfless act rewarding, his original altruism is reaffirmed and enhanced, or "renewed." His body is also "renewed" from his fasting. On the other hand, a starving man who feels compelled to steal food for himself serves as an example of the body imposing its demands on the spirit, with similar processes and parallels.

The engine driving renewal is change, and this engine never stops. Physically, we change every second of our lives from birth to death. We change spiritually as well. We are "made new" over and over again, like nature, but with an important difference: though the body is transient, the soul is eternal. The body and soul, through our free will, both receive and impose change for a purpose and meaning we determine. This process does not end until the day of our funeral, when the body and soul are severed. At that point, the final renewal of the spirit takes place when we return to God the soul He gave us, and He then does with it as He sees fit. Thus do the temporary shell and the eternal spirit interact constantly within the process of change. This is renewal.

Despite perception to the contrary, a sense of renewal is not a single, identifiable event in life. The process of renewal and change never ceases. However, it also does not manifest itself with uniform intensity or frequency. Like the ocean tide, the process is continuous and cannot be halted. But the tide has high and low points, eddies and currents, and varies according to weather and season. It occasionally has enormous waves that wipe away everything in their paths. So it is with life events and renewal. The process is always underway, but not always in the same manner. This variable experience of change permits us to break it up into meaningful events or series of events.

A positive sense of renewal can come from events not altogether pleasant; conversely, things we enjoy may renew us in ways we do not welcome. A man attacked and robbed on the street could choose to react in many ways. If his assailant is arrested and punished, the victim might feel a sense of renewed justice despite his traumatic experience. Conversely, if the victim finds the robbery intolerable and then seeks out and murders his attacker out of a thirst for revenge, he has imposed a negative renewal on the event.

Very often there exists no correct or "right" way to think about the vicissitudes of life, because experience remains subjective for us all. This applies whether the event is trivial or earthshaking. Does the man out walking his dog on a cold December morning marvel at the beauty of sunlight sparking off the snowdrifts, or does he curse the fact that he has to be outside shivering? The choice, effect, and renewal are all up to him.

Sitting in front of the television news in our living rooms, we cannot hope by ourselves to stop wars, end political persecution, or relieve famine-stricken refugees. Yet we can take comfort in the fact that no event is *completely* outside our control. Any event of which we are aware, no matter how remote, involves us in at least a passive sense, through its effects on us. That response might be spiritual, in praying for the famine victims, or it might be physical in joining and/or donating money to a relief organization. It could simply be emotional, when we pick up the telephone and share our experience with a friend. All these actions renew us, even if we do not recognize that fact. Even a simple feeling of empathy for the victims is a manifestation of the event within ourselves and connects us with humankind.

To feel "renewed" by any experience or activity, we must reflect on it. Most of us find it hard enough to manage the practical details of everyday life without pondering lofty, abstract spiritual issues. We may crave the feeling of renewal but find it elusive at best, ironic at worst, as in Solomon's observation: "What has been, is what will be … there is nothing new under the sun. Can one say of anything, 'look, this is new?'… I have seen all the things that are done under the sun and have found everything to be futile, a striving after wind." (Ecclesiastes 1:9-14). Yet, deriving a sense of meaning and purpose in one's life is the very thing that allows us to succeed in spite of the obstacles in our paths, and, therefore, understanding the concept of renewal could have no greater practical importance for us. There can be no renewal without purpose, and no purpose long endures without renewal. They exist in duality, and they progress through the medium of change.

The task before us then becomes one of placing change into meaningful context, and for this God has given us all guidance. Being imperfect ourselves, we cannot always successfully apply the lessons of faith to our lives. But when we bring all our weight of reason, passion and spirit to bear on such questions, very often we will indeed find some meaning and feel renewed thereby. Here, then, the role of faith in renewal cannot be challenged, for it serves as our beacon in a world dark with doubt.

Rather than an event which simply happens to us, in the final analysis renewal is a decision we make. Going back to France in 1919, the ex-soldiers felt bitter and resentful of nature's seemingly indifferent beauty. They also had a sense of helplessness in a world whose madness and infamy they had no ability to control. What they did not realize at the time, though some did later, was that God had given them the ability to control the reality within themselves; He also allowed them to play a part, however small, in modifying the effects that terrible war had upon the world. Nothing can be changed, affected, or renewed unless each individual, through the free will of the spirit, decides to do so. It is when we do this, and only when we do this, that we are renewed, rising anew from the ashes of the Phoenix.

JOSEPH B. HEIMER lives in Grand Rapids, Michigan. He attended the University of Dayton and currently works with mentally ill adults and children. Besides poetry and essays, Joseph has also completed a full-length novel in the fantasy/sci-fi genre.

March 27

grilled the last fish in the freezer
august sockeye from legoe bay

rose pink flesh full of oil—
fuel for the long journey never made

i carry the carcass down
return it to the sea   where

it will travel to crabs, gulls, dogfish
and the tiniest of critters, plankton

and, eventually, other sockeye.
passing through, into.   becoming.

just like us.
just like it has always been.

LUTHER ALLEN explains, "I write poetry because it is the form of expression that comes closest to making sense of experience and because I have to—it is how I make my place in the world. I have avoided poetry courses, workshops, and poetic academics because I wanted to develop an authentic voice." Allen grew up in New Mexico, studied biology and geography in college, and now lives in the Northwest where he designs houses for a living. March 27 comes from a 365-poem manuscript about nature/insight/perception entitled "The View from Lummi Island."

III. Healing

First Swim

August '63

While birds
hundreds, no thousands, of Hitchcock's
seagulls and blackbirds and crows
flooded the screen
knocked off women's hats
bashed their beaks into car windows
pecked at eyeballs and skin
I floated on my back in Fish House Cove

and the salt held me up
and I wasn't afraid
suspended like that
in my sister's hand-me-down suit
weightless and free
staring up at the wide blue sky
at the one white gull circling high above me.

Born and raised in mid-coastal Maine, HELEN HASKELL REMIEN now lives in Michigan's Upper Peninsula where she and her husband have raised two sons. She received her master's degree in creative writing from Northern Michigan University and has recently published a book of poems, *Wild Ground*. She teaches yoga and creativity workshops, writes stories and poems, performs as a storyteller and has designed and will soon open Joy Center, a sanctuary for yoga, dance, and workshops celebrating our creative spirit.

Come to the Edge

You cannot make steel until you have made the iron white hot in fire. . . . Our painful experiences are not meant to destroy us, but to burn out our dross, to hurry us back Home.
—SRI GYANAMATA

I'D JUST BET THE PARTY I COULD DRINK A BOTTLE OF SCOTCH in five minutes. I already had a couple of quarts of beer in me—it was *de rigueur* to oil up for a party—but I was feeling the need for some hard stuff. We'd beaten a football team we hadn't beaten for twenty years.

My teammate bolted upstairs to steal a bottle from his parents' liquor cabinet. Free booze and a fist full of bills! Everything was going according to plan.

In moments he was back with the bottle. I was at the center of a chanting crowd, about a hundred of us crammed into the basement rec room. I was nervous: I'd only chugged pitchers of beer before.

Someone held up a stop watch. I upended the bottle, opened my throat and chugged.

Five minutes later, my eyes tearing, my stomach screaming, I raised the empty bottle aloft.

The crowd burst into applause. I felt sensational. The girls were all over me. Nobody had ever seen anything like it. It was just as good as having scored the winning touchdown. Better maybe. In fact, this was the best party ever.

For about twenty minutes.

Then the opposing team crashed.

I don't remember any of it too clearly, but apparently their captain and I exchanged words. Shoves. Suddenly we were fighting. I have hazy recollections of wrestling him to the floor, turning the ping-pong table into kindling.

Everyone was shouting to take it outside. The whole party mobbed out the basement door. A steep flight of stone stairs led up to the back yard. He stood at the top waiting for me. I charged up after him.

The next thing I remember were stars: icy splinters of pain. The coward had kicked my head into the stone wall.

I fell back down the steps. My nose was broken, my head gashed—blood everywhere.

He took off. I went berserk and tore after him. In the dark everyone looked like the guy. I wasn't taking any chances. I decked them all: fathers arriving to pick up their daughters, brothers after their sisters, neighbors curious to see what in God's name the ruckus was about. I smashed windshields, kicked in car doors, tore up bushes.

The cops arrived.

I started in on them.

They started in on me with billy-clubs. They had no effect; I was going to kill that guy. Girls were screaming. Parents were screaming. I was screaming. Lights flashed. Sirens blazed. More cops arrived. I kept swinging. They kept swinging.

The next thing I remembered was being dragged up the steps of the White Plains Police Station by the handcuffs.

I felt that!?

For the next couple of months I couldn't feel much of anything in my hands.

I lay in the cell bleeding, screaming, out of my mind with consternation and rage. How had this happened? A couple of hours ago I'd been the hit of the party.

The next day the cops cuffed me and kid-gloved me out to a squad car. Saccharin-friendly, they seemed worried I'd erupt again. Little did they know, a vicious hangover turns an enraged beast into a pussy cat.

I was committed to Grasslands, the state mental institution.

I was seventeen.

DID THIS MEAN I HAD A DRINKING PROBLEM? Forget it. It was the opposing team's fault for crashing the party. I was too young to be an alcoholic. When I got my shopping cart and ragged coat, and moved into my cardboard box, I'd begin to think about such things.

I was institutionalized twice more after that.

If there's a single reason most alcoholics die from the disease, die by the tens of thousands, it's denial: the inability to recognize that they have a problem, that they are, in fact, killing themselves (and everyone around them). They possess a near bulletproof shield against reality—a pathological ability to divorce themselves from the truth.

The deeper the bottle drags them, the tighter they clutch it.

The German minister and philosopher Reinhold Niebuhr, the man who conceived the Serenity Prayer, wrote this variant: "God grant me the serenity to accept the people I cannot change, the courage to change the one I can, and the wisdom to know it's me."

It took me nearly fifteen years to glance in the existential mirror—and admit, ever so grudgingly, that I had a problem. I was the last to see what had been acutely obvious to everybody else. I'd totaled nearly every car I'd driven, ended up in a bloody altercation at least once a month. I was thrown out of every watering hole I drank in, every school I attended, some of them twice.

It took a third trip to an institution to finally open my eyes.

In the midst of a bad binge in New York, I suddenly realized I was so far gone, I'd lost the ability to stop. The beast had me in his jaws, halfway down his throat. I was powerless to prevent him from swallowing me whole. If I didn't check myself into a hospital, there was a good chance I would drink myself to death.

When I was released a month later, I was a changed man: chastened, terrified. This thing was more insidious than I'd ever imagined.

This time, I was determined to keep the beast caged. I tried everything I could think of. Just drinking beer. Just wine. Drinking after 5 PM. Weekends only. Running until I was half-dead. Lifting weights until I was nauseous.

Nothing worked.

Every morning I'd crawl out of bed determined to stay sober and by noon, I'd be wasted again. Noon, heck, usually within a half-hour of arising. Any good drinker learns rather quickly that the best way to cure a hangover is with another drink or drug.

I kept telling myself: *I'll get over it eventually. I'll learn to drink reasonably. Outgrow the compulsion.*

But you can't outgrow alcoholism. Even if you're not drinking, it's in the back room lifting weights, hitting the heavy bag, preparing to take you down the moment you reach for a drink. After a while, I couldn't function without getting loaded. I had to get high to get out of the house; then, just to pick up the phone. Eventually I got to the point where I even got loaded to meditate.

That's addiction.

IN THE LAST INSTITUTION, I'd been introduced to a self-help program. They were convinced the solution to addiction was spiritual:

Paul Klee.
*Tightrope Walker
[Seiltaenzer]*
Lithograph, 1923.
CNAC/MNAM/Dist.
Réunion des Musées
Nationaux / Art Resource,
New York. Musée
National d'Art Moderne,
Centre Georges
Pompidou, Paris, France.
Digital image
©2008 Artists Rights
Society (ARS), New York /
VG Bild-Kunst, Bonn.

"One drunk talking to another" could actually help a person stay sober. Maybe so, but to me it was one loser leeching off another. I could do this on my own.

I marched back to the Catholic church. Every morning I dragged myself out of bed for 8 AM mass. I flirted with hair shirts, beds of nails. I visited monasteries all over California, gave serious consideration to joining each one.

I kept drinking.

I shifted my gaze Eastward. I tried Buddhist meditation. I sat cross-legged until my legs screamed. I tried Yoga meditation, lifting my eyes to the third eye until I was worried I'd end up cross-eyed. I tried Sufi dancing—spun myself sick. Anything to get the dragon off my back.

None of it worked.

I tried fasting. All spiritual traditions touted its potential for purification. And God knows I needed purifying. At first I did just a day or so. When that didn't do it, I kept extending, up to ten days at a time. I'd starve the demon out of me.

Often a few days into a fast, sometimes a few hours, I'd get overwhelmed by something. Invariably nothing more than an unreturned phone call, a broken dinner date—It's always the major things that do us in, right?—and reach for a beer. Just a beer; no harm in a beer. Just to take the edge off. The problem is that an alcoholic's brain chemistry is so skewed that whatever he takes to dull the edge, only sharpens it, while he crosses over into oblivion.

In no time I'd be wasted again. (Nothing like an empty stomach to promote a gorgeous buzz.) Once the beast is out of his cage, it's a Herculean, if not impossible task to get him back in again. Einstein said it best, "Insanity is doing the same thing over and over again and expecting different results."

I needed stronger measures. I decided to try fasting in the mountains. Hard to find a beer on a ten-thousand-foot peak. I'd read the autobiography of the great Lakota medicine man, Lame Deer. He'd been a terrible alcoholic. He considered his vision quest to be the beginning of his recovery. The Lakota believed that a vision quest—four days in the mountains without food or water—is a way of offering the Great Spirit the only thing He doesn't have already—your flesh. They felt it attracted a guardian spirit; no warrior was permitted to engage in battle until he'd experienced this rite of passage.

I thought why not give it a shot.

I drove down to an Indian reservation in San Diego County and set up camp overlooking the Anza-Borrego desert. It was a lot drier than I'd bargained for. Within an hour I was parched, despondent, desperate for water.

Ninety-five hours to go; I was dying already. I'd never make it.

Fasting for four days without food is a breeze compared to a single day without water. There were many times I'd have sold my soul for a sip. I prayed. I obsessed. I prayed some more. Too often the prayer was, "Please God, let this be over soon."

All I could think about was water, Coke, icy lemonade—better yet, waterfalls of beer, lakes of iced champagne, cases and cases of ice-cold vodka.

There were times God was so close I could almost feel His whiskers. Other times, I felt utterly abandoned. One thing was for certain: they were some of the most fervent days I'd ever spent. I'd pound this damned addiction out of me somehow.

I'd read you get close to death on these things. No one had mentioned that it was because suicide seemed like the best way out. But I had to get sober. If it killed me, at least I'd have died sober.

I did a vision quest every year for a decade. Sometimes two.

I'm convinced that those quests were the beginning of the end of my drinking. I have no idea whether I actually attracted a guardian spirit or whether the waking dreams I had counted as visions. I do know this: ninety-six hours of fasting with God—however conflicted—is bound to change something. After each one I felt uplifted, enriched: it was as if I'd emptied myself to fill myself with light. There was an almost palpable connection with Spirit, an inner voice I could trust.

Still, I was doing what's known in recovery as white-knuckling it. It means exactly what it sounds like: gritting my teeth and holding on tight. Every alkie has tried it, and even if it works, it only succeeds in creating another, equally insidious type of misery—a profound disconnect from oneself and everyone else. Without the camaraderie of "one drunk talking to another" the alcoholic festers, turns inward, his untreated rage and resentment invariably drives him to drink again.

When white-knuckling failed to do the trick, I devised a program of my own: The Marijuana Maintenance Program. The heck with those twelve steps. I honed mine down to one—keep it simple right? *Take whatever chemical is necessary to keep from drinking.*

The insanity of progressive alcoholism.

It didn't take more than a double digit IQ to see that my program was fatally flawed. But did I see it? Of course not. It worked just fine. I wasn't drinking was I?

AFTER A DISASTROUS, COKED-OUT New Year's Eve in New York, I finally hit bottom. Maybe it was time to check out those stupid meetings. There was no way they were going to work. None. But I'd tried everything else. I had nothing to lose.

So reluctantly, belligerently, in fact, I tried one. I was definitely not going to stick with them. I wouldn't even drink with these losers. I was just checking it out as I had Buddhist meditation, Sufi dancing, monasteries. Just another lost cause.

After a week or so, I noticed I wasn't drinking . . . or drugging. Hmmmm, maybe there was something to this. Impossible. These people were too weird.

I kept going.

I'd been sober about a month, when I arrived at my writing partner's apartment in West Hollywood at 6:00 ready to work on a screenplay as scheduled. He was in bed. He insisted I come back in an hour. I'd driven nearly an hour in rush-hour traffic and was more than a little annoyed. I was in no mood to drive a moment longer, but I figured I'd take the high road and seek some spiritual sustenance.

I consulted a little book that listed meetings of my self-help group. There was one on Crescent Heights Boulevard not far away. I drove over. It was a church. But it appeared to be locked up. Now I was really annoyed. Deny an alcoholic a spiritual solution . . . well, deny an alcoholic anything really . . . and you've got a problem.

I consulted the book again: found another meeting already in progress—and sped off. It was a low-slung community building on Holloway. But it too was locked tight.

I stood there, fuming. What I really wanted to do was drive back to my partner's apartment and beat the hell out of him.

But again my higher self prevailed. I decided to try to meditate. I drove down Sunset Boulevard to a church I knew. I parked, walked up the long flight of steps only to discover that, you guessed it, it too was locked.

God was definitely not on my side that day. This damn sobriety thing was for the birds. How valid was an organization that listed meetings, then didn't hold them? Just as I'd thought, they were a bunch of lame losers.

I needed a drink. A joint. Something. Bad! That scared me.

I decided it was time to do something I'd sworn I'd never do: call another alcoholic. I'd met a guy at one of the meetings, and we'd exchanged numbers. I'd done it just to be polite. I knew I'd never in a million years actually call him. Did I mention I wouldn't even drink with those idiots?

But here I was eating crow, marching up to the phone booth, half-hoping the guy wouldn't be home. Talk about nuts!? Here's a potential solution to my problem, and I'm hoping it doesn't work.

He answered. Damn. "Hey Mike! How you doing?"

"OK. Who's this?"

"Duane from the meeting."

"Hey man, good to hear your voice. I was wondering how you were doing? Still sober?"

"Barely."

"Me too!"

We shared a semi-hysterical laugh that was way out of proportion to the situation (or maybe it wasn't). All I could think was: *this guy is whacked.*

But at that moment, I swear it, I was cleansed of every bit of rage and self loathing. It was as if a waterfall of light had broken loose all around me.

My God, maybe this "one drunk talking to another" business really did work. Maybe these people weren't so crazy. Maybe it was me.

I hung up feeling fine, better than I had all day. All month in fact. I got back in my car. An hour had passed. I drove back to my partner's and instead of beating him to pulp, sat down to work.

I'm not saying sobriety was this easy. It wasn't. That phone call was a mini-miracle. I need miracles to be convinced. Nothing quite like that ever happened again. I found I could turn things around by talking to another alcoholic, but it generally took a whole lot longer. That call was the carrot. Eating it took a whole lot of endurance, patience, and, at times, excruciatingly hard work.

It was the turning point in my relationship to the group. If I could get that kind of relief for one phone call, I'd give it another few weeks.

Weeks turned into months. I still wasn't sure I wanted to be there, but I was struck by the fact that I hadn't had a drink or a drug since I started going to meetings.

There's a wonderful acronym for ego: Edging God Out. It wasn't until I gave up trying to do it on my own that I got the grace to stay sober. It wasn't until I succumbed to "weakness" that God gave me strength.

Guillaume Apollinaire, the great French poet, summed up the whole journey with this: "Come to the edge, he said. They said: We are afraid. Come to the edge, he said. They came. He pushed them and they flew."

There I was at ten thousand feet . . . no idea how I'd gotten there.

I'm nearly thirty years sober now and sobriety even at its worst is paradise compared to the slow torturous death of alcoholism.

There's a wonderful story in the life of St. Theresa of Avila, who one day, exasperated with the endless challenges and difficulties in her life, cried out, "Why Lord?" God responded, "This is the way I treat my friends." The ever witty St. Theresa replied: "No wonder, My Lord, you have so few friends."

NOW THAT I'D LOST MY SKEPTICISM of my newly adopted self-help program, it was time to actually work it—time to pay back my debts, rub out the record.

I'd pulled a scam on American Express for years. Whenever I needed money I'd figured out a way to double up on traveler's checks.

I wasn't sure how much I owed them, but since I used to pull the scam regularly, I knew the amount was considerable. Ten thousand dollars, maybe more. I figured I'd get started with five hundred.

I headed over to a bank and ordered a cashier's check for that amount. I didn't have a checking account yet. I was thirty years old and had never had one. If there's one certainty about alcoholism: it stunts your growth.

While the teller drew up the check, I happened to glance at the clock. It was 2:50. Typically, I'd just make it before closing. At that moment I got a distinct rush, a buzz akin to a long pull on a strong drink. It felt like God trying to tell me something. I had only ordered the check, and I was getting this kind of juice! Man these steps were something!

I got home to discover that at exactly 2:50 a call had come in from a casting director, asking me to "Do him a favor." (Hollywood lingo for getting you to accept a small part.) It was for the TV show the "A-Team."

The offer for the day was five hundred dollars!

I sent the check off to American Express along with an explanatory letter and flew back to New York to visit my family for Christmas. I returned to a stack of mail. I noticed a letter from American Express.

Panic.

What if they wanted the whole amount? What if they were pressing charges? I was badly jet-lagged and not exactly keen on spending the next few years on the run.

I put it at the bottom of the pile.

Finally, I opened it. It read: "Dear Mr. Tucker, since this matter is over ten years old, our computers no longer have a record of it. We do appreciate your honesty. Here's your check back and please continue to use American Express."

If that's not redemption, I don't know what is!

Oh, and the "A-Team" turned into a boon. They used my scene in another episode. I didn't have to do a thing. Just collect two paychecks for one day's work.

I'm still getting residuals.

DUANE TUCKER is an ex-pat American: screenwriter, critic, and poet. He toured for years with his one-man show on John Muir, one of the earliest and most poetic of environmentalists. In the *Embracing Relationships* issue, Chrysalis Reader published his account of how that play led to romance, marriage, and settling down to a new life in Canada. In a previous career in Hollywood, he appeared in over seventy films and television shows. He also wrote several movies, two of which were optioned. His poetry has been widely published. University of Baltimore's *Passager Magazine* voted him poet of the year 2002. He has reviewed theatre for the *Hamilton Spectator* and written art criticism for *Canadian Art and Border Crossings.*

A Place to Play

STANDING IN FRONT OF THE VOLUNTEERS' MAILBOX in the Monrovia, California, police station, I read the complaint letters in my hand. One is to the mayor of our city of thirty-six thousand. Citizens had written protests saying, "Small children from another neighborhood are playing on our front lawns. They keep coming back. Please do something about it." A note clipped to the letters says, "Give to Ralph."

I wonder, *Shouldn't this case go to Juvenile? I don't work with children. Gang members, yes. But not little kids.*

I call Mrs. Salazar, one of the letter-writers. "My name's Ralph. I'm a volunteer with the City Police Department, calling about your letter to Mayor Bartlett. May I visit you this morning to discuss your problem?"

"Yes, please do."

SESMAS STREET DEAD-ENDS AT AN APARTMENT COMPLEX. Her attractive house is on a short cul-de-sac branching off Sesmas.

Mrs. Salazar speaks kindly, "The children come from the apartments down the street and romp about on our lawns. They look to be from four to ten or twelve years old, some barefoot. They need a place to play. They run off when I open my door."

I suggest, "We need to have a meeting between the children's parents and you homeowners. I'll call you."

"I'll help from this end."

BENEATH A STEEL STAIRCASE four children play on the concrete. The street dead-ends a car-length from the stairs.

The kids are obviously untended. Three wall-to-wall buildings have six units each, three up, three down, eighteen units. I look around for trees or grass. None. Not even any dirt. All concrete.

The growing family of children in the Neighborhood Recreation Program at Julian Fisher Park in Monrovia, California, was featured in the *Pasadena Star News*, August 15, 1992.

The mailbox panel tells me the manager is in Unit 4. The steel stairs ring like a dull bell beneath my feet.

"Yes, my wife and I manage the apartments."

I explain the problem and ask, "How many kids live here?"

"Maybe twenty or so. Some run loose. What can I do? Nothing."

"Will you come to a neighborhood meeting to talk about the problem?"

"Sure. Where?"

He's cooperative. "I'll call you."

"Okay."

I need the tenants at the meeting, but they can't be invited by the police department. There may be a few real losers here, maybe even guys on parole. "Will you notify all your tenants that they're invited by Monrovia Neighborhood Watch?"

"Okay."

Six homeowners show up with lawn chairs. The apartment managers and one parent come over with blankets. It's a bust.

The next morning I ask the manager, "May I have a list of your tenants and the number of children in each unit?"

With the list in hand I knock on doors and interview a dozen adults to ask if any kids are signed up for summer events. After an hour on the premises I realize there is little parental concern. I see bumps on this road.

There's a monitored park a mile from Sesmas Street. I learn there are children's' activities, free lunch, and Friday bus trips to places like museums and Disneyland.

I check out the fenced park. Kids. Green grass. Swings. Counselors. Everything. Lunch tables are grouped neatly in the shade beneath a large roofed area.

A slim black girl, about eighteen, a whistle on a cord around her neck, sees my approaching clipboard and meets me with a smile at the open gate.

"I know you, Ralph," she says with a strong, sweet voice. "My mom's Block Captain on Los Angeles Street. My name's Edison."

"Hi. I've seen you at the meetings. Who should I talk to here about bringing a new batch of kids in?"

"Me."

She's able, smart, attractive. I feel a spark of hope. "Do you have room for more kids?"

"Lots."

"Tell me what I need to do."

"You'll need a medical waiver filled out and signed by the parent. I'll show you one. Then bring the signed forms to me with your 'batch of kids'."

"Edison, you're a sweetheart."

"We'll take them tomorrow."

I wangle two dozen blank waiver forms from the clerks at Community Service, fifteen in Spanish. I go straight to the apartment manager with the forms and ask for help. He hands them out to his renters. Nothing comes back. Another bump on the road.

I type a short explanation in simple words about the park, the lunch, the counselors, and the Friday trips, then run off eighteen copies. The manager hands them out. The next day there are four sign-ups.

A day later there are a dozen forms all filled out. The kids on the concrete surround me with eager faces. But the parents are not able to transport their children.

I call Community Service. "We're ready to take twelve kids from Sesmas Street to the park. Can you arrange transportation?"

"Sorry, Ralph. No money. We can't help you."

Same with Parks and Recreation.

There's a small inner-city transit line. I call them. "Yes, we can do it. But you need a state-licensed person riding on the bus with the children."

Finding a ride for the kids is a major bump on the road. Dismayed, I go back to the park.

"Where are your kids, Ralph?" Edison asks.

"Here are the signed forms. The kids are ready, but I can't get them delivered here. It's frustrating."

"That's a shame." She takes a long look at my Trooper suburban parked nearby.

She's a very smart young lady, this Edison. She's knows a volunteer when she sees one. I yield. "They'll be here in the morning."

Three sit in the front with me, five in the back seat, and six in the rear, fourteen in all. They spill out at the park with squeals, running across the grass like water escaping a burst barricade.

"I'll pick them up at four, Edison, and deliver them again tomorrow."

THE NEXT MORNING I turn onto Sesmas to see a flood of children run from the concrete toward the car, filling the street with their flashing forms and excited cries. Quite a sight. More sign-ups are coming. Nothing should stop this.

Transportation is a major problem, one I'm not equipped to deal with. One expert problem-solver I haven't seen yet is the City Manager. I send a fax.

That does it! Like magic. The kids are taken care of.

Some days later I enter the station on my way to Crime Prevention when the officers and clerks, to my astonishment, applaud my passage.

"What's going on?" I ask a sergeant in the protection of the division office.

"Your idea to bus kids to parks this summer really took off."

That gives me a warm feeling. Each little challenge had been met and overcome. "I wonder how many there are now. We had fourteen kids on my last trip."

"Ha, you'd better catch up. There are over four thousand kids in Los Angeles County entering your program in hundreds of parks. You are definitely Big-Daddy around here."

I think of the complaint letters about the Sesmas Street kids and Mrs. Salazar's comment, "They need a place to play."

It was really her idea.

Known as "Ralph" to several thousand Neighborhood Watch members, he served for nine years as a volunteer with the Monrovia Police Department Community Policing Division while receiving commendations from city, county, state, and U.S. Congressional offices. RALPH EMERSON PRAY holds degrees from the University of Alaska and the Colorado School of Mines and has traveled widely in his work in mineral-property evaluations. Dr. Pray has taught engineering at the university level and has been writing for publication for fifty years.

Grace

I LIMPED DREADFULLY ACROSS THE CHURCH PARKING LOT. I didn't think my hip was anything serious. But every time I got up from a long sit those days, I'm afraid I resembled the hunchback of Notre Dame. Bent over, hobbling, gasping with pain until the stiffness wore off—pretty pitiful for a young woman.

It wasn't for this pain that I'd driven to the healing service. In fact, it wasn't for me at all. I came for Frank, someone I barely knew.

Frank's not his real name, but he is a real person. Our families both went to an Episcopal church in Eugene. He had a beautiful wife, two young boys, a senior position at a bank, a great big moustache, sparkling elfish eyes, and the most upbeat personality you could ever meet. He also had an aggressive form of cancer clawing its way through his jaw. His doctors couldn't operate because surgery might ruin the nerves in his face. So they were doing their best with radiation and chemotherapy, but it didn't look good.

I didn't like to bring up healing and miracles with someone I didn't know well. Even if we did go to the same church. Miracles and all that, well, it can be a touchy subject. So when I heard about the healing service, I had to work up my courage to call.

Frank wasn't home, so I told his wife about it. A Catholic priest was coming, Father Peter Mary Rookey. He traveled around from church to church, holding services where some people were miraculously healed. He was holding a service at St. Helens Catholic Church in Sweet Home, Tuesday night at 6:30.

She was awfully polite. She didn't think Frank could go. He had something else he had to do on Tuesday night, but thanks so much for calling.

Okay, that was awkward, I thought, as I hung up. I could see, though, why they wouldn't want to add one more thing to days already full of doctors' visits, pain, nausea, lab tests, terror, and grief.

95

Oh, and trying to live as normally as possible on top of all that. Even though he was sick from radiation treatments, Frank still dragged himself to work every day and still coached his son's baseball team. He did it for his sons, so they wouldn't be so scared—to normalize their lives upturned by cancer.

I knew miraculous healing was unlikely. I mean, how many people did I know who had been instantly cured at a church service? None. But I still wished he would go. Because what if it worked? What if there was a chance for some miracle, and he got better?

And then I thought, you know, people take communion on behalf of others. I could just go to the service myself, tell God I'm standing in for Frank, and then see what He would do. It couldn't hurt, I figured. Why not?

So that Tuesday my husband watched the kids as I drove alone to the service. It was the hour's drive, in fact, that made my right hip hurt so. Whenever I sat for a long time it did this. I drove up into the foothills of the Cascade Mountains to the little logging town of Sweet Home. Why Father Peter Mary Rookey would come to such an out-of-the-way place, I had no idea. But the service didn't lack for people. When I limped up to the entrance, greeters directed me to a big basket of cheap, white, plastic rosaries for people who forgot theirs. Or, let's be honest, for people who didn't own one. I did own one, a gift from my Catholic sister-in-law, who I'm sure had prayed for years that I would see the light and become a Catholic too. But I didn't think to bring mine, so I borrowed one of theirs. I figured if I could make my way through communion, I could probably do the rosary thing too.

Let me just apologize right now to all you Catholics, especially all you Catholic priests, for the countless times I went to mass even though I wasn't Catholic. I confess that I'd snuck into plenty of Catholic churches and pretended I knew what I was doing so I could take communion. *Lord, I am not worthy to receive you, but only say the word and I will be healed.* I knew most of the words and would move my lips through the rest, hoping no one would notice.

But that night I wasn't prepared for all the Hail Marys and the Our Fathers. I'd never worked my way around a rosary before and, just between you and me, it did seem to go on a very long time. I knew the Our Fathers already, better known in my church as the Lord's Prayer. You know, *Our father, who art in heaven, hallowed be thy name.* But not so much the Hail Marys. I knew the beginning. *Hail Mary full of grace, the Lord is with thee. Blessed art thou among women and blessed is the fruit of thy womb, Jesus.* The rest I tried to lip-synch. Something, something, something, *pray for us sinners now and in the hour of our deaths.*

The church was packed. They'd put folding chairs all around the sides and the back and in the narthex, everywhere they could while still leaving space for people to walk or wheelchair around. Even so, every seat was taken, so I stood at the back.

For the first few Hail Marys anyone would have seen at a glance that I wasn't a member of this church—or any other Catholic church. But I got it down, let me tell you, because I had so many opportunities to say it. We went all the way around the cheap, white, plastic rosary, for goodness' sake. So by the end, I could say a Hail Mary like a pro.

The stained-glass windows dimmed as night came. The church became dark and hushed. They lit candles.

Father Peter Mary asked if anyone saw angels in the church. A boy sitting a few pews in front of me raised his hand. Father asked if anyone smelled a scent of flowers. The boy raised his hand again.

Not me. I didn't notice anything out of the ordinary. I stood very still in the back, watching everything, praying for Frank. Praying for God to heal him.

Frank and I once participated in a *Faith Alive!* weekend at our church. We were in the same small group when we each reviewed our personal spiritual development. We all wrote down some thoughts about our lives on the paper they handed us. Then we summarized the highlights with the others in the group. I'd had adventurous parents, spiritual seekers, but, alas, it hadn't led to a brilliant spiritual life so far. Mine was mostly a muddling sort of life and not an especially joyful one back then.

Then Frank talked about his life. His was all good, all upbeat, no complaints here. And he wasn't just saying it. He was that sort of a guy. Very positive, very can-do. That was before the cancer.

It makes you wonder about that power-of-positive-thinking thing, about prayer, and why it works sometimes and appears to do nothing at others. Maybe it's really all about karma, about receiving what you give. Maybe it's about receiving what you need to grow, like it or not. Maybe it's just about viruses and the complexity of the human body. Or maybe it's about all those things.

But then, sometimes, maybe it's about grace.

Where I stood, baseboard lights shone softly on the carpet so people could find their way. Strangers stood on either side of me, rosaries in hand. The men of St. Helens Catholic Church took turns standing up from their pews and leading prayers in strong, proud voices. We went through the rosaries bead by bead. Apparently these Catholics didn't just walk up to God and ask for something. They worshiped for a good long time first.

*Anne
McGinley*

Portrait of a Woman.
Attributed to the Saint
Louis Painter, Roman,
active ca. 290–310 AD.
Tempera on wood,
10⁹/16 x 6¹³/16 in.,
ca. 300 AD. Saint Louis
Art Museum. Gift
of Mrs. Max A. Goldstein.

All at once I felt a tingling in my right hip, like an electric current. While I stood quietly against the back wall, after the Hail Marys and the Our Fathers and all had really gotten rolling, but before the actual healing part of the service began, I felt the buzzing exactly where my hip had been paining me. When I looked down, wondering what it was, I saw nothing but my ordinary, familiar body. It vibrated for a moment, and then it was gone.

Finally Father Mary Peter told people they could come up for healing. He explained the logistics. We'll start with the front rows and work back; the ushers will let you know when it's your turn. Those of us who could stand should go to the altar rail. He said he would pray over each of us and mark a cross on our foreheads with his thumb, which he would have dipped in holy oil. If you felt the urge to fall, don't resist it, just let yourself fall. Strong men from the community were there to catch you, so you would be safe. Just give in and let yourself fall back.

So people lined up standing at the altar rail, and Father made his way along the rail, touching each person, speaking to everyone. And people fell like Douglas firs before the power of Mount St. Helens. They just fell backwards, into the arms of the waiting men of Sweet Home, who lowered them to the floor. He moved down the line and people fell one by one, like dominos. They sprawled all over the floor before the altar rail. He moved down the rail, from my left to my right, and then returned to the beginning, where new people had stepped over those on the floor and waited for him, lined up at the rail. I'd never seen anything like it.

A small church choir sang behind Father while he did this. Since I was at the very back, I had a long wait before my turn came. I watched all this and thought, *Oh Lord. This is not my style. This must be what it's like to be slain in the spirit.* Or as my hairdresser says, slayed in the spirit. Oh, yeah, she told me, I was slayed in the spirit before. She went to an Assembly of God church. But here I was in a nice, traditonal Catholic church, and I'm watching people fall down up there by the rail. And I'm thinking, *Oh Lord, I hope I don't have to do that. This is really not my style at all.*

At long last my turn came. I had serious reservations. Falling to the floor just seemed unnecessary and so . . . so . . . undignified. But I told myself, *I'm doing this for Frank. I'll do it for Frank. If it works and he is healed, it will be worth it.*

So I got in line with all the ill, all the desperate, and the faithful who were hoping for a miracle, and I made my way slowly up the center aisle. The church was full of lit candles, the choir sang and sang. At the altar I stepped carefully between the arms and the legs of the people lying there, and I took my place toward the right end of the rail. *God,* I said, *I'm here in Frank's place. So when my turn comes, please heal him.*

The church is dark now, and hushed, even with all the people moving through it. The church choir is still singing behind Father. I watch as he works his way toward me, down the long line of people standing at the rail. I see many of them fall backwards into the strong arms of the men of Sweet Home. *Oh Lord,* I think as they fall. But then I remind myself, again, *I'm here for Frank.*

Now Father is standing in front of me, speaking to me, and making the sign of the cross on my forehead. I stand with my eyes closed while he does this. When he finishes making the sign, he doesn't move on. He stands there, his thumb still pressed against my forehead. Now he is pushing against it. I think, ah, he really wants us to fall. But I stand. And he keeps pushing me backwards, harder now. So I think, *oh, what the heck,* and I let myself fall backwards.

A man behind me whispers urgently in my ear, there's no room! There's no room for you to lie down! Too many bodies on the floor of St. Helen's Catholic Church. But I'm letting myself fall now, and I figure it's up to this guy to deal with it, whoever he is. I feel him catch me and lay me down gently on the floor. So I guess some space must have appeared.

I'm not slain in the spirit. But I lie there for a bit just in case it will help Frank.

I return the white, plastic rosary as I leave. I get in my Aerostar and drive to Main Street and then onto Highway 228. I negotiate the long, curvy road up through the foothills and then down into the farmland near Brownsville. I wonder if anything happened for Frank. I pass through miles and miles of grass fields and smell the dairy farm as I pass it in the dark. I merge onto I-5 and drive south another 21 miles before I get off at the Eugene exit and make my way home.

I park in the driveway and get out my house key as I walk to the door. Then I realize: my hip doesn't hurt—at all. I am not gritting my teeth, I'm not bent over, I'm not limping. It feels perfectly fine. I just got out of the car, and I am walking with ease, straight and strong.

A week or two later, at Frank's next oncology appointment, his doctors were amazed that the tumor had died suddenly and completely. All that was left was an empty, shriveled shell.

Everyone who knew Frank rejoiced that he was well. Really, it was miraculous, wasn't it? people said. The way the cancer just died like that? I rejoiced with them. How good, how very good it was that he would live to raise his sons, love his wife, and shine his light in the world.

In the weeks and years that followed, my hip did not bother me at all. It was healed. I never told Frank that I'd gone to the service for him. Our families both moved on to different churches, and when I see him, we are practically strangers.

But I know what happened that night. In his great need, healing came to him. And in a quiet moment at the back of a church it came unexpectedly to me, too.

ANNE McGINLEY is a development research analyst at the University of Oregon. She enjoys camping, her English cottage garden, and playing on Oregon's rivers with her husband and their two teenagers.

WILLIAM KLOEFKORN

Tea

.

*It's good to have poems that begin with tea
and end with God.*
—ROBERT BLY

God knows it's good also to have poems
that begin with God and end with tea,

especially if the tea is hot and your fever
waning, you a day or so earlier so sick

you wanted to write an ode in praise
of death, sweet sweet death, wanted to be

not yourself but Walt Whitman, say,
that chef expansive enough to include

death as an entrée, or more likely a
dessert, but before you managed

to put pencil to paper the fever eased,
and now you find yourself sitting alive

and upright in a padded chair, easy the
chair, easy the way the one who serves you

brings relief, her hand steady as she
places the cup on the small table beside

you, aroma of something cinnamon
and divine rising to find you, and verily

it does, and you snap your pencil like a twig
while saying to hell with that ode

to death, to hell with dying, to hell with
Walt Whitman and his foolish expansiveness,

to hell with all things not blooming, and
you bring the cup to your lips

and sip, liquid hot as the center of Hades
against the tongue, liquid delivered

by someone you truly care for who
truly cares for thee—call it whatever name

you choose to believe in, you fortunate
little apostle, as long as you call it tea.

WILLIAM KLOEFKORN's most recent books are a memoir, *At Home on This Moveable Earth* (University of Nebraska Press) and a collection of poetry—with reproductions of paintings by Carlos Frey—*Still Life Moving* (Wayne State Press in Nebraska). He is published widely in journals and periodicals, among them *Prairie Schooner, Harper's, Puerto del Sol, Georgia Review, Iowa Review,* and the *Virginia Quarterly Review.* A book of poems, *Out of Attica,* is forthcoming from Backwaters Press in Omaha. He lives in Lincoln, Nebraska.

Nothing Vanishes

A garden is not for giving or taking. A garden is for all.
—FRANCIS BURNETT

ONCE AGAIN, the same voice woke me from depths of soundless sleep, "Now. Rise. Come to this place. Come." I rose, my body all the while resisting leaving the companionable warmth of my bed to climb to the cemetery at the top of the hill in dark November cold. My yellow lab, who usually leapt from his bed, now just stirred slightly, opened an eye, then closed it. Too early even for him.

I shivered and dressed, ran my hands through my hair, and turned on the flashlight. I was indebted to the silence of the house and to separate bedrooms. Grateful my shuffling didn't wake Everett, my husband of less than two years, this man who told me he loved me because my life seemed so manageable. I knew differently. I scrabbled through my closet for warm clothes—shirts, pants hung askew, a few scattered on the floor. This chaos mirrored the reality of the past ten years of my single life—my life before our marriage. I'd cared for and buried five family members—my late husband, both parents and two aunts—and raised two sons alone.

I knew if Everett saw me awake and dressing at three o'clock in the morning, walking to the cemetery through the black night to wrap my arms around the crepe myrtle tree, a torrent of questions would spill from his lips. I was even surprised at myself, at this ritual. Yet, night after night, this urge pressed me on.

Everett looked quizzically at me last week when rocks dug out of the garden by Agatha, our Cherokee landscaper, were left piled in a mound where they were dug. He didn't understand at first why we couldn't get rid of the stones. They were messy, disorderly, and distracted him, he said, when all he wanted to see was the beauty of wild-

flowers. I explained that Agatha believed moving the stones disturbed their place of rest in the garden. He stared at me. Then a small, "Oh, I see," slid from his lips. I knew he didn't see at all, but he trusted me. I also knew he'd become upset if he learned it was the nightly trips to the cemetery that left me tired and foggy during the day.

I pulled the wrought iron latch on the garden gate forged with black laurel leaves, swung it open, and set the flashlight on the river rock wall sides that formed the base for the fence. A half moon illuminated the flat brass markers on each gravestone. In the row closest to my feet lay my two aunts, side by side in death as they had been in life. In the second row were my parents, and furthest away, in the first row, my late husband, Henry. At each grave I bent down, ran my hands across the name in a greeting and blessing. Behind me a circle of native shrubs—holly, quince, and bayberry—defined the land that had once been an open field. I'd bought the shrubs believing they were dwarfs, a species that were compact and would grow close to the ground. Yet, each had outgrown its space, so there was no longer room between plants. An unbroken circle of green growth flourished here, encircling the graves.

"DON'T GO, DON'T GO, DON'T GO . . ." But Henry, my husband of twenty-two years was already gone. I stood over his bed. Then, I leaned over him and kissed his cheek. I slid back into the chair next to the bedside, cupped his cooling fingers between my palms feeling the gold of his wedding band warm slightly between my hands. Even though the hospital suggested he do so, Henry refused to remove his ring. "No need. I'll be home in a couple of days."

A nurse arrived on soundless feet, leaned over my slumped shoulder. "Stay as long as you like. Take your time with him." She stilled the machine with two clicks and left. The only breath in the room was mine and with each exhalation the word *loss* echoed in my ears.

I watched the stillness of his body in death, intently hoping for slight eye movement, any small, shallow stirring of his chest. Henry remained lifeless, unmoving and unchanged. His body affirmed the truth. I sobbed and watched his skin turn from pale pink to gray. Time vanished with my grief. I couldn't believe what was. It just wasn't acceptable that this six-foot-two, 200-pound, vital, take-charge man was a lifeless corpse. All of me worked to reject what I'd witnessed. Still unbelieving, still trying to distill hope from the truth, I waited for him to open his eyes.

Henry was supposed to die at home in the presence of his family reading the daily *Wall Street Journal,* listening to the whir of the fax machine spit out numbers for his latest business projects, while

Opposite:
Guenter Wehrhan.
Untitled (detail).
Pen and ink, 1989.
Collection
of Eric Hoffman,
LaPorte, Indiana.

enjoying the welcome distraction of his sons running in and out of his home office. He was supposed to wear his favorite gold wool blazer, the one that kept his body temperature just warm enough when chemotherapy left him chilled. The plan for him to die at home, did not, however, include a critical case of pneumonia that raced through his already weakened immune system, sending him to the hospital. He died, dressed in a thin institutional gown in a place where no one knew him. A part of me understood he'd been well taken care of by strangers here, as much as medicine could do.

But this was not what he chose, what we wanted. But then, his death wasn't either.

I shifted in the straight-back chair next to him, knowing I had to leave him, not being ready to do so. To leave now seemed disloyal, final. There was nothing left, but still I was unable to leave his side. I stroked the length of his forearm back and forth, longing for the comfort I'd always found touching him. I nestled my head against his arm wanting one more moment of him, just one more. I felt a hand touch my shoulder. Two women friends arrived to drive me home through the black November night.

The drive home was filled with images of Henry's body being zipped into a black body bag by strangers who would not know what he needed. My mind was still married to him, occupied with the way he liked his laundry done, the way he drank his coffee, the way he slept with his blanket just so over his lower legs. Later that night, I awoke with a start, my pillow wet with tears, hoping the funeral home was treating his body gently.

The following day I arrived at the funeral home feeling as if my feet were sinking in soft sand. My body was as ungainly, as inaccessible as my feelings. I entered the parlor disguised as a cozy living room to conceal the business of making agonizing decisions. I glanced down and looked at my abysmal blouse, one I hadn't known I owned. It hung loose over dark brown slacks that fell in folds onto my weather-beaten brown shoes. I felt like a splatter of mud standing next to the funeral director's impeccable black suit and highly polished shoes.

"Where would you like Henry to be buried?" His voice was soothing, smooth.

I looked at him blankly. Words seemed difficult to form. My mind required the work of mental gymnastics, and I barely had energy to stand upright. Henry's death was sudden, and we hadn't made necessary arrangements thinking there was always time, always time. We'd only lived in our house three months. I knew of two cemeteries in town. Both were located on busy streets, one across from the high school, the other along a four-lane highway. That wouldn't do. I still felt ownership of his care and shouldered the responsibility to make right decisions for him. Then, the haze cleared, and I remembered what Henry said about the highest point on our property, "It's so beautiful, so peaceful. This would be a good place for a cemetery."

So I, a tenderfoot from Chicago, transplanted to the mountains of Western North Carolina, built a cemetery, a sacred space. A local stonemason built the wall of North Carolina river rock. A blacksmith welded black wrought iron laurel leaves in a pattern I drew for the gate. I researched the history of the area and discovered it was called Sweet Woods, so to the stone wall near the gate I attached a brass marker and scripted it "Sweet Woods Garden."

The process of planting Sweet Woods Garden became an emptying experience. As I found myself on my knees in touch with black dirt, my mind became unburdened, and all disquieting thoughts spilled into furrows left by roots pulled from weeding. Several hours of gardening left my fuzzy mind calm and clear. My body felt the good kind of tired that hard physical work produced. My clothes, smelling of sweet, black soil, cleansed me.

Gardening led to more planting throughout the property. Growing flowers was a satisfying promise: a plant took root and bloomed, as it always did under Agatha's careful tutelage. Flowers produced color and vigor year after year. I strolled among the gifts of the garden scattered at my feet to find foxglove with its tall lavender spikes, columbine with blooms in pink and yellow, azaleas splashed orange, pink and candy stripe, sturdy daisies, and a multitude of day lilies pledging their bounty. I'd stand at the end of a full day of labor, back stiff, sunburned neck and arms, on this ground I'd tended, first with a sense of obligation, now with a feeling of connectedness. I'd found my new partner in the earth, this soil beneath my feet.

Over the next ten years four more family members died and were buried in Sweet Woods Garden, one every two years. When grief ensued, I grieved as I gardened following the same ritual. The cemetery became a place to meditate. It was the place to go for the comfort and the continuity of long-term family relationships. They were all there and seemed eager to speak with me as I developed the ability to hear.

As I spent more and more time in this space, my mind cleared. Messages came about how to raise my two sons alone, how to manage the myriad everyday issues that arose as I lived my single life. I'd ask questions and wait, sitting on a stone bench under the dogwood tree within the circle of shrubs. Shiny green holly leaves mixed with the coarser threads of evergreens mirrored my own struggle to mix my rough grieving life with the new. Giant bumblebees drank nectar from fuchsia bee balm behind the dogwood. Monarch butterflies stopped to rest on the top of the gate between feedings on the last few blooms of azaleas. All nature seemed to welcome me and create a place for me.

One summer a raccoon climbed the crepe myrtle tree and died, its leg wedged between two close-growing branches. Agatha pried the small, stiff body from the tree and buried it in the woods. She recounted the story and explained that this sacrifice was a cleansing ritual. "How blessed you are!" She grinned. I'd not told Everett about the raccoon or the ritual. The crepe myrtle then shed its bark to cleanse itself of this sacrifice. It now stood perfectly formed, its bark smooth as gray clay, top to bottom. The tree had been a scraggly stick until that summer. It was now a guardian tree, its symmetry perfect and tall, outlined against the Carolina sky.

The crepe myrtle stood fifteen feet tall with several large, heavier branches supporting small ones. The smooth, gray bark glistened in the moonlight. I pressed my body into its trunk, feeling its unwavering strength. I wrapped my palms around a smooth, thick branch, then stood still beneath the silent sky. Within seconds the tree emanated energy. Vibrations began in my fingers, traveled the length of my arms, through my torso, and down to my feet. I found myself mouthing names of family members now living, now needing comfort and healing. If I'd stepped outside myself to watch, I'd feel like an empty-headed, old woman. Yet, these actions felt altogether natural. It was as if being here was the yield, the harvest for years spent planning and tending Sweet Woods Garden. And now, with the knowledge of the guardian tree, the cemetery became my compass. During these nocturnal visits, my focus shifted. No longer were my children, husband, church, or my books the anchor. This place was my center.

As each family member was lowered into his grave, my life seemed to develop a new rhythm and harmony on the wave of the loss. Loss, burial, grief, and renewal became my landscape. The pattern of living and dying was like planting. I became one with the process of growth, life, death, and renewal. A new, sweet-smelling melody was imprinted on me as surely as the genetic code for the color of each rose in the garden. Nothing vanishes. I looked outward to the living, healing testament of the garden. Nothing vanishes. Nothing.

Before moving to the mountains of North Carolina, KAREN LAURITZEN worked in Chicago as a medical social worker. Several of her short stories have been published in *WNC Woman Magazine.* Her short story, "Alter," won third prize in its annual short story contest in 2007, and the fictional characters in "Alter" will also appear in her novel in progress, "All Her Worldly Goods." She has co-authored a nonfiction book with Ruth E. Lycke, *Hope, Help and Healing: Traveling for Treatment in China.*

Men's Retreat

The second morning of the Men's Retreat I called my wife.
"I don't know about this," I said quietly, mouth cupped over the phone.
"It's more like a Pentecostal Revival than a Catholic Men's Retreat."
"What do you mean?" She sounded disappointed.
"I mean there's all this singing and spontaneous prayer
        and tearful testifying and . . .
"And men I hardly know are hugging me!"
"Just be open," she said.
"Don't be uptight. Give it a chance. Just be open."

She was right. I gave it a chance. Loosened up.
And found myself enjoying the experience.
I discovered quietly courageous men who had overcome
        clinical depression or alcoholism
        to forge for themselves and their families
        decent lives of sobriety and service.
I discovered the joys of singing
And the value of spontaneous prayer.
I read the Bible in a new way.
And I discovered something about myself.

On the last evening while Father was thanking us for being there,
And I was congratulating myself for "opening up,"
The team leaders quietly left the hall.
And when Father said that while we were on retreat,
Our families and friends were praying for us – at home and in the chapel—
I thought, *That's nice,* and saw the team leaders come back,
Each carrying a small branch from a tree.
Fluttering from the twigs of each branch were dozens of pieces of paper—
Like blossoms.

Father said that these were prayers, or "love letters,"
Written to us by the third graders of St. Barnabas.
I smiled condescendingly.
I could hear the third-grade teacher telling her class:
"Now, children, write a nice letter to someone on the Men's Retreat.

"Tell him Jesus loves him. Write neatly."
As a branch of fluttering love letters got to my table, I suddenly realized—
My daughter, Karen, was in the third grade at St. Barnabas.
Someone who would kiss me goodnight every night
On the left hand, left cheek, right cheek, right hand
And only then go up to bed.
Somebody who loved me unconditionally.

And I saw myself for what I was—
A fatuous fool unworthy of such love—
And wept, reaching to touch
One particular note.

CHRIS BUNSEY taught high school English from 1960 to 1990, coached tennis and cross-country running, and taught at Cuyahoga Community College. He has been published in *Nerve Cowboy, Sidewalks, The National Catholic Reporter,* and *The Heartlands Today.* Chris has staged a play based on love sonnets of Shakespeare and Elizabeth Barrett Browning. He leads writers' workshops and is currently writing character portrayals of the many volunteers in the Diocese of Cleveland, Ohio, for a monthly newsletter.

Beyond Grief

Writing Circles for Healing

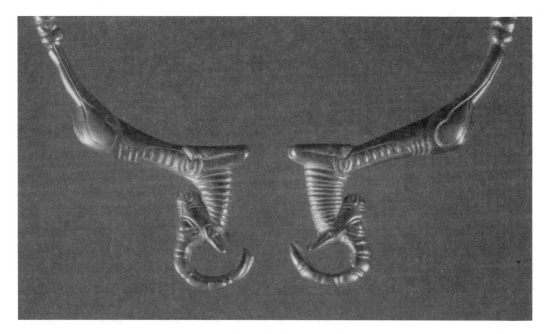

OF ALL THE IMAGES THAT HAUNT ME about the memorial, the one of distributing Sam's ashes is the clearest. The ashes were picked up from the funeral home in a cardboard box. The services we had chosen were the simplest and cheapest. I recalled how in Santa Fe, the funeral director had taken on this task himself; Michael's ashes were distributed into five ceramic pots we had picked up at a pottery store, each alike but each one hand-thrown and thus unique. The director had warned us not to let anyone know we had divided the ashes, especially the priest who was to conduct a mass dedicated to Michael. The prevailing faith in New Mexico is Catholicism, and I learned that they believe it is wrong to separate the ashes of the deceased.

We smuggled my portion over the Mexican border to leave on a hilltop above the town of Magdalena, the first town where we used to stay overnight whenever we traveled into Mexico. As his closest three friends and I stood in a circle of cempasúchil petals, the large golden marigolds used on *Dia de los Muertos*, I felt Michael's journey had ended mercifully, and he was freed at last of his suffering.

Bracelet (detail).
Gold, Persian,
Achaemenid period,
$3^3/4$ x $3^9/16$ in.
ca. 550–331 BC.
Saint Louis Art Museum.
Funds given
anonymously.

I wanted to be the one to divide Sam's ashes. I knew that his father was in no shape to do it and neither was his fiancée. We were all in a state of shock. Later it could be diagnosed as post-traumatic stress. But I had been through this experience three years previously, and so I was the one—I knew what to do.

Pouring Sam's ashes with a big spoon into each container was my last chance to touch him, the baby I had nursed at my breast, the little boy I had comforted in my arms, the man I had taken out to lunch to ask him how it felt to be a father. I had chosen containers that looked like tall Egyptian urns with a patina of antiqued silver, bought at World Market. I had anointed his face with cherished olive oil brought from Israel and wept until my insides felt turned inside out. But it was the mechanical tasks, the holy tasks, the candles lit by the boys who were to be his stepsons, the photos compiled into a collage displayed during the memorial, the dividing of his ashes, that kept me moving through the nightmare.

I could no longer pray or write, the two things that sustain me spiritually and emotionally. I was furious at God, at the challenges life had thrown me, at the twist of fate that had left me a widow followed by the death of my youngest son. It felt unfair that just as I was coming out of my grief over Michael, I was faced with another loss. But this time, the loss was different. With Michael, we all knew his bipolar illness was making him suffer; we understood and honored his decision to end his life. With Sam, it was a shocking and unexpected blow. *It should not have happened,* I seethed. Most of all, I was angry at myself—that I had not seen it coming, that I did not have an intuition the day it happened, that I had not shown up uninvited to his house and changed the sequence of events: the drinking, the argument, the rage, the fatal spontaneous decision to end his life.

Later, a woman who had lost her little daughter squeezed my hand as we talked and wept together. She told me she thought I wasn't supposed to know, I wasn't supposed to stop it, horrible as that thought is. There is some reason he was meant to go, she assured me. I believe that no one can go before his time, yet in this case. . . . It felt like a mistake. A stupid decision made under the influence of alcohol and a fight that escalated out of control. I can't shake that thought, no matter how many psychics, shamans, grief counselors, spiritual advisors, and grieving parents tell me otherwise.

I asked others to pray for me and with me. My first appointment was with Owen Kunkle, chaplain of the hospice center where I had been a volunteer. I told him the news and asked him to pray on my behalf. I just can't, I explained. He understood, took my hands in his, and we made a prayer together. He with words, me with my aching, tormented presence.

Over Thanksgiving, I spent three days at the Christ in the Desert Monastery. I needed the silence, the sense of sacred place, and the company of those who still have their faith. I chanted the hymns in Gregorian along with the guests, stumbling, biting my tongue in places where God came too close, letting tears spill when they must. He had scorched me, and I was gun-shy and grief-weary. But when the monk who was the guest-master listed all those being prayed for, he said my name aloud instead of just "the guests who have joined us." I wept tears of gratitude. I was too angry to speak with God yet, but I was grateful that someone was jogging His memory: I am still here, broken, scarred, exhausted but here.

I took a long walk to the place where we had thrown Sam's ashes into the Chama River. A flood of memories accompanied me. I had camped here when I was pregnant with Sam, and I had felt angry and betrayed then, too. I was living in a commune and didn't want another pregnancy so close to my first. I wanted to be involved in community activities that required my talents and attention, not taking care of another little one. But of course, the minute he was born, I fell in love and have loved him every second since. My walk was another goodbye on a string of goodbyes. It was just too hard to let go.

How dare God ask so much of me? To not only give up my child but at the time when I was finally turning the corner of my grieving over Michael, when I was writing poetry, performing, traveling, and making the connections to launch me into the next phase of my life, the phase of no longer being a caregiver but an artist. My dreams crumbled into dust as I dragged myself through each day of work. I no longer had inspiration or desire.

The journey I took was a journey to the bottom; the dark night of the soul was more excruciating than I had ever imagined. But I *had* a spiritual foundation even if I couldn't access it. Years of meditation and prayer had given me this foundation. Years of learning traditional healing from the elders and how to communicate with the river, the wind, the rocks, and the earth. My support systems, Word Dancers, a group of women writers, and the women in my Moon Lodge, learning to call in the directions, drum for the spirits, create rituals, pray in a sweat lodge. The times spent on my knees in churches in Mexico, the candles lit, the pesos dropped into a can. The faithfulness of being a hitchhiker, dependent on the kindness of strangers and the whims of fate. The poems written and spoken to the hearts of my audience. These upheld me even when I felt I had sunk too far to ever return. I thought I had given up everything when Michael died. It felt like descent to the underworld to flay off my skin at times, but never before had I doubted that I had cultivated a relationship of loving father–mother Creator and devoted daughter. Losing my faith was like losing the will to live.

And yet, in a part of me, I knew there was a gift here. I knew somewhere in the filth and despair was a jewel. That knowing was the result of spiritual practice, even if I couldn't imagine what that jewel might be.

My oldest son asked me to come to Minneapolis to help with childcare. It meant leaving my friends and support groups, but I was ready for a fresh start and a new perspective. And didn't I say I wanted to spend time with my grandsons while they were little? I had vowed never to live in such a cold climate. I could not imagine being shut up in the house eight months out of the year. I shuddered, remembering my experience of the arctic blast. The year that Sam turned twenty-one, we went out to dinner in weather that was ten below zero. Despite the long underwear on top of tights under my velour dress, I was chilled to the bone until I warmed my blood with the wine we ordered.

IN DECEMBER, I accompanied my friend Liz to Arc, a contemplative ecumenical retreat center forty-five minutes away in the woodlands of Minnesota. The first snow had slushed into ice, but the retreat center had three fireplaces, kept the teapot filled, and served lovely vegetarian meals. She was there to attend a board meeting, but I was free to hang out and explore the woods, the expansive spiritual library, or just sit in silence in my room.

The main building looked like a large log cabin. We were just in time for the first formal introductory meeting, and as each person spoke, I sank into a palpable sense of tranquility and kindred spirits. Afterwards, as a snack of home-baked bread, jam, and fruit was set out, we were shown to our rooms. Each room was arranged comfortably with its own sink, bed, desk, and rocking chair. I sighed as I settled in for the two days, spreading out my notebook, journal, and poetry books on the desk, putting my toothbrush on the sink, and draping my sweater over the arm of the rocking chair. Later, munching on bread and fruit, we conversed quietly with the other guests and members who have chosen this simple and rustic lifestyle away from the bright lights, fast paced traffic and congestion of the city.

I was tired of confiding in people what had happened to me and to my child and knew that Minnesotans would never pry. I was free to disclose however much I wanted to. The sympathetic sounds that someone made or the attempts to hide shock and dismay grated on my soul and yet, it could not *not* be said. I am a poet accustomed to revelation more than secrecy. I am still on the quest for answers and I find them everywhere, even in the heart of a stranger as we lean closer in empathy. Everyone has a story, I soon discovered. Everyone has a story of tragedy and grief, and finds courage to go on, keeping afloat their raft on life's seas.

We gathered in the small chapel for vespers. In a Quaker-based tradition, we sat by candlelit silence in a contemplative circle. In the deepening silence, thoughts of Sam came immediately to the surface, and I closed my eyes. As I sat in silence, suddenly it came to me: *the promise is that there is life after death.* For me. My life will go on. In ways I have not predicted, in places I had vowed never to live.

Before dawn, we were awakened to join in the chapel again. This time there was an empty seat next to me, and I felt Sam's presence. I shed grateful tears for this sign that I have been waiting for, longing for, the knowledge that we are still connected and part of each other, that death does not keep us apart. For this moment alone, I was glad I had come there. The anger was cracking, melting, like icicles dripping from the eaves. Later, after hours spent alone in my room, reading, thinking, allowing the changes to settle deeper into my bones, I went outside for a breath of fresh air, the sky a pristine blue, icicles melting, and air invigorating. The path into the woods was still covered in snow, so I was only able to navigate a circle around the building but I breathed in the fresh cold of winter woods, alive for the first time since Sam had died.

The idea of writing circles came to me soon after that. The idea began as a desire to continue the writing process that happens in a group setting and not finding a group that I could join. I began to think: I have the experience of going through grief; I have facilitated writing workshops for years; I have been a hospice volunteer; and I have been trained to listen to others' stories. My passion for words began to come back to me. I was writing poetry again after intermittent and sporadic attempts that crashed into the walls of my resistance. How could I honor Sam? How could I make meaning out of his death? Here was a dream to propel me out of the pit into something I could offer, something true to my own soul. I could facilitate writing groups for people who have suffered or are suffering. I can help people to access their deepest thoughts and fears. *I have been through it all.* And I am still here, shaken, worn, but wanting to embrace life again. Only not for myself, but to make sense of what felt senseless, to give meaning to what felt like a mistake.

The pages of business plans and networking ideas were interwoven with hugs from the little boys and shoveling wet sand in the sandbox. Something was born, something struggled to shake its wet wings in order to fly. All the prayers that had carried me to this point were heard. I began to write down my own prayers, asking for strength, the grace to make it through my days with a gift in my hand instead of the memory of pain. I began to meditate by candlelight, gently, not pushing myself, when I feel strong enough to withstand the grief and the disappointment that still arise.

Recently I was reading an article in the *Writer's Digest,* and a writer said that the thing about writing is that you have to be able to accept rejection. You make a *submission* to a magazine or a publishing house. And that is what we have to learn to do, submit. Surrender. Give in. Not the same as giving up at all.

Writing Circles for Healing is a writing support group to write our way through loss, grief, illness, trauma, and life-altering transitions. Writing in a group setting can be therapeutic as we share what is deepest within us. Using simple techniques of spontaneous free writing, we access our inner healer. By sharing our stories with focused attention, we validate our experiences and enter into a deeper awareness of inner abilities and strengths. We transform what may be painful into something profound and full of meaning. We gain fresh perspectives on our lives to find courage and hope.

WENDY BROWN–BAEZ is the creator of Writing Circles for Healing. She is a performance poet who has performed nationally and in Mexico in cafes, bars, galleries, bookstores, peace centers, and private homes, solo and in collaborations. In 2004 she released her poetry CD *Longing for Home.* She was the recipient of a 2008 McKnight grant to teach a bilingual writing workshop in El Colegio Charter School.

CATHERINE MUNCH

Evening Birds

It's an evening of summer birds, so beautiful
I'm not surprised when dark doesn't still
their talking. They lightly stir the hedges,
every tree limb, every telephone wire sways.
They sing themselves alive, plentiful and eager
in a night filled with the whirr of insects.

Hares wait inside the treeline out beyond the yard,
not yet swimming through the grass.
They wait for me to leave,
to go into the silvering house to sleep,
their day's story within a candle's breath of ending.
Trails, paths laid through the tall grass
wait for the hares' trespass,
wait for their explorations,
wait for moonshine and the chill of dew.

I'm caught at the back door by an evening so beautiful
I'm not surprised when dark doesn't still the birds talking.
They're plentiful and eager
in a night filled with the whirr of insects.
I sing myself alive, the hedges lightly stirring,
every tree limb, every telephone wire sways.

Oak and aspen disappear into twilight.
A woodthrush emboldened by camouflage,
a sparrow hawk by his rapture, sing themselves alive.
I still the screen door's swing.
my heart thrums to the man
watching beyond the tall grass,
waiting in the treeline for me to beckon him home.

Hares wait, not yet swimming through the field,
wait for him to leave,
wait for us to enter the silvering house,
wait for me to lose my voice in sleep.
Our day's story is within a candle's breath of ending.
Paths, trails laid down in the tall grass
wait for the hares' trespass,
their sweet explorations,
wait for the hares to slip through
moonshine and the chill of dew.

CATHERINE MUNCH has lived from Bangor, Maine, to Santa Cruz, California, where she now teaches American Sign Language at Cabrillo College. Cate has performed signed interpretations at the National and American Folk Festivals. Her articles, short stories, and poetry appear on National Public Radio, in the *North American Review, the Writer,* and in other journals and magazines.

Jerusalem

of the passage through
Eternal Death! And of the awaking to Eternal Life.
This theme calls me in sleep night after night, &
                                    Ev'ry morn
Wakes me at sunrise; then I see the Savior over me
Spreading his beams of love & dictating the words of
                              This mild song.

—WILLIAM BLAKE, *JERUSALEM*

SO WILLIAM BLAKE BEGINS HIS VISIONARY WORK *JERUSALEM*. Boldly he claims that Christ co-authors the work. Indeed, he draws a picture of Christ as original author and himself as merely the scribe, taking dictation. That claim is what makes him a visionary author, relying on spiritual revelation in order to write at all.

I first read these words in 1970, and I decided then and there that I too would be a visionary, receiving spiritual truth and transmitting it. In me, however, the decision was a form of hubris, and I took a hard fall.

The problem began when I tried to take a shortcut and have visionary experiences fueled by alcohol and drugs. Instead of visions, I got increasingly disturbing hallucinations. My excesses began to have a negative impact. I managed to hold things together long enough to get my degree and begin teaching at a university. But increasingly my drug and alcohol use took over my life.

For five years I struggled, either resigning or being fired from job after job. One day I came home to an eviction notice on the door. I was without resources, material or spiritual.

I began a new phase: life as a homeless woman. Not knowing the ropes, I carefully studied my cohorts and quickly learned their tech-

Sister Gertrude Morgan. *New Jerusalem.* Acrylic and tempera on cardboard, 12 x 19 in., ca. 1970. Collection of the American Folk Art Museum, New York. Gift of Sanford Smith and Patricia Smith. (1986.21.1)

niques. These included how to panhandle, how to feed myself from dumpsters, how to find shelter in abandoned cars and under freeways, and how to run from street violence. It was possible to wake with nothing and nevertheless manage to get enough to drink (primary goal) and eat (secondary goal) each day.

I soon accepted the uncanny sensation of being invisible. As I sat on a ledge outside a market to panhandle enough for a bottle of wine, most people passing looked right through me, as if I were not there. We inhabited separate worlds, although we were close enough to touch.

This time period in my life lasted ten years. By the end, I was experiencing what Blake would call "Eternal Death." My nickname was "The Zombie," because I had lost the ability to form thoughts and to speak. I only awoke in order to drink myself into oblivion.

One night, I walked the streets of San Francisco with a small group of fellow homeless. We had a fight over whose turn it was to push the grocery cart containing our bedding and possessions. I refused to take my turn. Oddly enough, I thought it was beneath me to push the cart. The others took umbrage, and I felt the thud and sharp pain of being hit in the eye.

The next morning I had a huge black eye. The others were concerned because soon it would be time for my SSI (government disability) check to arrive. It was my custom to get the check, cash it, and spend it on alcohol and cigarettes for everyone. The party would last two or three days. When the money ran out, we wearily would return to panhandling.

Everyone pretended that someone else, an unknown villain, must have hit me. They were very solicitous and insisted I do no panhandling work that day but simply gather my bedding and rest. I did. Soon the others joined me, and we all passed out in Golden Gate Park.

I came to in the late afternoon and realized that something had changed. I felt as though a mighty wind had blown through me, rearranging me from the inside out. I looked at the bodies of my companions and thought, *What am I doing here? There is nothing holding me here. I think I'll walk away.*

I left the park. As I walked, I felt as though I were being guided by a female figure. She led me to a homeless shelter I could never have found on my own. Who was that presence? To this day, I have no idea. The Bible presents *wisdom* as a female figure. Perhaps it was she.

The next morning my check came to the post-office box I had rented. Instead of cashing the check and taking it back to my homeless cronies for a time of revelry, I bought a Greyhound Bus ticket to Los Angeles. From there I made my way to South Pasadena, where my mother and stepfather lived, to ask for help.

They were delighted to see me. My mother had been wakened through the years by nightmares in which I was being attacked or dying. She heard me calling out to her for help. Now, here I was. My stepfather, a recovered alcoholic, took me to sobriety meetings. Numbly at first, and then with increasing interest, I accompanied him.

Slowly and gradually, I began to heal. My thoughts, at first a chaotic jumble, began to clear. I realized I could write again. Haltingly, I began to converse. I learned that many people had been praying for my return. The female figure who led me out of a living death may have been the answer to those prayers.

It has now been eighteen years. I work as a college English teacher. It is a joy to guide each semester's new students and to help them hone their writing and analytical skills. There are always a few who share their hopes and dreams with me; I am part of their lives.

In the summers I take off. This is my time to focus on my own writing, which nourishes me. It is exhilarating to begin each morning with a blank page and fill it. Upon awaking, I find time for prayer and meditation. Then I come into the study to continue an ongoing conversation with Christ, which for me takes the form of an online journal. Next I begin writing. While I cannot claim, as Blake does, that Christ "dictates" the words, I do feel a sense of partnership.

I have moved from death to life. Today, I have a spiritual life and an active social life. I meet with friends for movies, meals, and sharing our thoughts, feelings, secrets. I have a satisfying family life. By my steady presence, I have atoned for abandoning them for a bottle.

Renewal comes each new day; it comes with the accumulation of good days into year after year of experiencing life anew. Why me? Of the scores of homeless who wander the streets, delusional and desperate, why was I led out of that death into new life? I am grateful.

Blake has written that a moment in time may open out into infinity. When I was led out of Golden Gate Park, I was given such a moment and took it.

DENISE BLUE is a former Woodrow Wilson and Ford Foundation Fellow. After the downward slide chronicled in this essay, she was able to rebuild a new life. Currently she teaches English at the community college level. She lives in Pasadena, California.

ANNE SILVER

Back on Path

Red bike, ready to mount,
because I'm as restless
as wheels, ready for the path.
Knots of metal chain
gear sprockets to wheels.
The bike and I know
how to get from tight curves
to downhill straightaways.
Nothing but calf muscles
balled and wedded to will.
In a flick of a downshift
I'm through with
the chemo ward's slick floors.
I'm back. Even if it's cold,
it's still lighter than when
I had to cycle through sand—
turning and returning,
standing high on the pedals—
bike ticking left-right-left
fills the spaces between
my teeth, cards flap
in the narrow spoke gaps,
messages to childhood.

Even though there are things
more frightening than getting lost,
the possibility of goodbye
or of someone saying
what I have cannot be fixed.
But it could, so I squint
straight ahead into the sun-
soaked sand parted
by the ribbon of cement squares—
visoring the sun with my forearm
to see what will welcome
me beyond the pier.

Widely published, ANNE SILVER was a winner of the 2004 Passager, City of
Los Angeles Cultural Affairs Department, "Sense of Site" and Red Hen Press'
contests. Her poem "Remains of the Day" was selected for the 10th
Anniversary Anthology of *Atlanta Review*—the very best from the decade.
The same poem, plus "Simple Dress," was also selected for *Death, Be Not
Proud Anthology* (University of Iowa Press 2005). She received a master's degree from the Instituto de Allende in Mexico. With a second master's degree
in psychology, she led workshops for people living with life-threatening ill-
nesses. Until her death in fall 2005 from breast cancer, Anne worked as a
forensic handwriting expert in court cases.

Experiential Encounter

SEE THE SKY REACHING FOREVER with a hard, blue hand. Meadow grass sways for miles under its glare. Over there, somewhere, is New York City. I know this, but I can't tell you who first told me so. I've wandered off my block. I've come to a dead-end on the street I am biking. I'm ten years old and not allowed to go too far. I've gone very far. I'm not lost, but the unending sky and miles and miles of green below me make me feel lost. Riding my bike, exploring, I had felt big, strong, older. Now, having dismounted and faced this part of the earth new to me, I have become so small—I may not be here at all.

In 1940, nothing stirred in the New Jersey meadows but muskrats, birds, insects, butterflies, and wild dogs. I can't see any of this, but I know they are there. The older boys tell stories on hot, summer nights about kids who wander into the meadows, never to be seen again, torn to bits by packs of wild dogs. I look apprehensively over my shoulder, but there is only an empty street. It is mid-afternoon. The sun illuminates everything with fingers that etch all the edges into purple. I know I'd better get on my bike and head home before my mother panics and I hear sirens. But I don't move. I am mesmerized by distance. I am hypnotized by all I don't know. How do I hold in my mind the wild scene below me, New York City somewhere on the other side, the street behind me, and the me that can grow large and small within a few minutes.

Trying to imagine the wild dogs in the green reeds, I find myself wondering about God. Why had God made this earth with scary things like wild dogs, unknown creatures like muskrats, and a girl who feels the need to ride away from her known neighborhood? Who now stands at the end of this never-before-seen street looking down on one boundary of New Jersey. Again I look as far as I can, trying to touch New York, and suddenly know: God created me out of loneliness. When God stood at the end of this street looking out, who was there to describe it to? Who was there to share the mystery with? Who was there to understand the connection with distance and reaching out for the unseen New York? *Me,* I say out loud. And immediately I feel ten feet tall again.

LYNN MARTIN says, "I've just turned seventy-three and have been a serious writer twenty-three years. My current love is collaborations. My goals for the future are a new book of poetry to be called "Talking to the Day" and an exhibit of my paintings and poetry to illustrate how they are connected."

IV. Life's Path

FRANKLIN HAY

Writer's Block

Not being in love is hell.
The sun comes up crooked
or not at all.
What does it matter
as the rain comes down.

Even a hurricane is ho-hum
as it eats its orange heart out,
silent and relentless
at the front door.

Gone is the Muse
with bare legs
and not a glance over her shoulder.
Boring, she yawns.

Next thing I know
there are only blank postcards
from Bombay, Majorca,
Costa Rica, and Cancun.

No word, no word, not a word.

I need a laugh across a room
that blinding light
heart-stopper of a walk.

Oh yes, love
can open the floodgates,

probably by accident,
but who cares

if I'm tumbled
and talking.

See LYNN MARTIN's biography on page 126.

Coming Through!

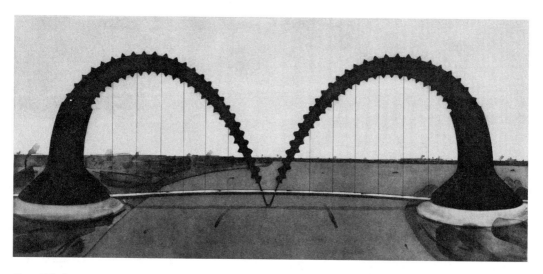

Claes Oldenburg.
*Screwarch Bridge
(State II).*
Etching and aquatint,
plate 23¹¹/16 x 50³/4 in.,
sheet 31³/16 x 57⁷/8 in.,
1980. Publisher:
Multiples, Inc., New York.
Printer: Aeropress,
New York. Edition: 35.
The Museum of Modern
Art, New York. Gift of
Laus G. Perls and Heinz
Berggruen in memory
of Frank Perls, Art Dealer
(by exchange). Digital
Image ©The Museum
of Modern Art/Licensed
by SCALA / Art Resource,
New York. ©Claes
Oldenburg, 2008.

TERRY WAS ABOUT AS BLAND A STUDENT in my freshman composition class as you can imagine. But I do remember his response to an in-class, warm-up assignment, which was to write his own obituary for the newspaper. "Your death will occur fifty years from today," I told the class. "What will be said of you?" This assignment was supposed to help students to visualize with specific details, but I also wanted them to realize that they created their lives everyday and to consider how they could live more intentionally now so that at the end they would have something to look back on with pride. Contemplating one's death should motivate a person to seize each day instead of letting life simply happen.

Most students dutifully cited their future children and grandchildren, future travels to exotic places, and future life trophies. But Terry wrote:

On May 6, Terry S_____ of 124 Walnut Street died from a lack of excitement. He suffered from the affliction his entire life, and doctors stated they had never known such a case to last seventy-one years. He is survived by no one and leaves behind only an old gray house that is the neighborhood eyesore.

His accomplishments were few and dull. He was the foreman of the litter-cleaning crew at the local minor league base-ball stadium. A company spokesperson estimated he lifted 1.5 million times his own weight in peanut shells while employed there. He woke every morning except his final one, helped an average number of old ladies across busy streets and once shined the shoes of a drunk. He had nearly completed his college degree when he realized he did not know why he should bother, so he quit. No memorial services are planned.

I was moved by Terry's honesty and vividness and complimented him for saying what many people vaguely sense but seldom admit. I also spoke to him about his deep resignation. He was not upset, certainly did not seem depressed in a clinical sense, for he arrived each class on time, prepared and groomed and was neither downcast nor glassy-eyed. His was a philosophical vision of the blah-ness of human lives and the mundane ends to which we whirled in time's eddies. He saw clearly the half-lives most people live and accepted such a fate as one accepts a sunset or rainy day. A handful of people might shoot up like rockets from the crawling mass of humanity and light up the darkness for a moment, but he knew he would not.

It was hard to deny that his vision accurately described many lives, but I rebelled at someone young, intelligent, and healthy being so devoid of hope, an adventuresome spirit and zest. It seemed to me that by anticipating boredom, he caused it. He ought to be leaping into the years ahead like a deer on a May morning, not burrowing into mud like a toad expecting to wait out winter. I told him, "You can do more with your life."

"How?"

"You can finish your degree. You're quite capable."

"I know," he agreed. "Then I'll pick up pieces of paper instead of peanut shells."

I laughed at his tartness. "Do you have a girlfriend, Terry?"

"Mmm. Sure."

"Wouldn't she mourn you?"

"I guess so—for a while."

So it went. After we talked, he returned to being the quiet guy near the back of class and wrote nice 'B' papers the rest of the way—enough to do well but nothing that would incite the professor to request another chat. He passed through my life over twenty years ago and never contacted me later, nor have I heard a word about him. I saved his paper and my scribbled notes, and sometimes I wonder how he has made out now that he approaches the halfway point to that possible obituary. Did he graduate? Had life been as dreary and flat as he predicted, or did he discover something worthy of passion? Did he still think enthusiasm was a hollow reed that would blow over in the first storm? I'm sure he would be surprised to know that of all the other students in that comp class who have vanished into my memories' dark crevices, I carry only him with me, for his one flight above the ordinary.

In college as in life, vitality and resignation do not seem predictable based on logical cause and effect. Consider a second student. James's legs looked dehydrated in his wheelchair. They'd never leaped, run, or even stood. But James wore work boots laced to the top as though he were prepared to haul skids onto the loading dock at a moment's notice. He operated his wheelchair like a forklift, zigzagging through crowded halls with reckless abandon, ramming doors open. Students stepped aside smartly when he whizzed past, his head tilted forward as if into the wind. A few grumbled about the handicapped "maniac." When he wheeled into class, he bumped chairs as he K-turned.

Sheltered and isolated at home for most of his thirty-two years, James had been at his mother's mercy. She loved, pitied, protected, and controlled him. Regardless of current hairstyles, Mother cut James's hair short and slicked it back, since he could not lift his arms high enough to brush stray hairs from his eyes. He loved his parents but was imprisoned by their care and fought furiously to create an identity for himself. He refused to be the person his parents saw. They were afraid to let him enter the world and only reluctantly allowed him to attend a "center" three days a week to learn "life skills." That whetted his desire, and James lobbied for six years before they finally allowed him to enroll in college.

As most therapists will tell you, the expectations and encouragement of my first student's family, friends, and high-school teachers should have been first-class tickets to success, yet all Terry saw were peanut shells. He used only half his effort and even less of his potential passion to pursue these expectations. On the other hand, James had to smash down his parents' and teachers' walls (he had no friends). He should have gone nowhere without encouragement and a support group. Yet he surged with enthusiasm, and his energy seemed far greater than his flesh's capacity. It makes me wonder if "You can't" is a stronger motivator for some people than "You're supposed to." Can crisis, solitude, and struggle be more our allies than we think?

Since he could not raise a hand high when he wanted to speak, James signaled with a looping waggle of his head. As he spoke, his head flopped backward, then caught and slowly settled forward before jerking backward again. His voice clacked, not in a stutter, but with excess precision that sharply enunciated each letter. His ideas were equally meticulous; he supported each point with evidence to make himself invincible against retorts. If another student disagreed with his viewpoint, James cut the argument to shreds, often adding that certain positions were "id-i-o-tic" or "lame." I had to remind him to be courteous. I'm not sure he really understood the concept of courtesy—perhaps because life had shown him so little.

I worried that he set destructively high standards for himself that would poison his future. 'A' minuses were weak; 'A's were ordinary; he needed 'A' pluses to repair his broken world. More often than not, that is what he earned in his classes. His writing was not imaginative, for he scorned metaphors as silly fluff, but his style was direct, bold, grammatically perfect, and hard-hitting. He conveyed information and argued cases with overwhelming evidence. One day I heard a classmate who had just been skewered by James mumble in the hall, "Sure, he's smart; what else can he do but study?"

The blind harshness of the comment shocked me. Didn't this boy see what James had done? Didn't he see that we were *all* handicapped in our own ways and that James was setting an example for all of us? We only become fully alive when we defy our limits. Terry was correct that the implacable forces that shape our ends eventually hem us in. But James gritted his teeth, rammed into them, and learned he could shove some aside, at least for a while. When the smothering pillow of routine and time is lowered over our faces, that is the moment to summon our passion. We do not have to cooperate with death's agents.

To get to his next class after mine, James had to wheel down a long hall to an elevator, rise a floor, then race down three long halls back the way he came. So as the clock approached the hour, he prepared like an eager sprinter in the starting blocks. He did not look on any of this as exhausting, unfair, or stressful; rather, it was exciting just to live at full throttle. He shot out the door as soon as released. I handed him his papers first and offered to let him leave a minute early, but he refused. "I might miss some-thing," he said.

"Have I said anything worthwhile the last minute?" I asked with a smile.

"Not yet," he said, "But you might get luck-y." He grinned back—his first smile.

One December day when six inches of wind-whipped snow piled up, and a third of my students did not make it to class, James arrived a few minutes late—his only lateness. He banged his wheelchair furiously into the other desks. "It's okay," I said, making a palms-down motion with both hands. "Don't get upset."

"They have not plowed the side-walks yet," he fumed. "How am I sup-posed to nav-i-gate my chair in that?"

"Maybe you need snow tires?" I suggested. A second smile flickered on his face, but he doused it. Jobs should be done or else.

Everything should be what it was supposed to be and done properly. There was no room for excuses or mediocrity in his philosophy.

James, of course, made the dean's list and the honor society. This seemed to please him, although he did not relax when he won these official stamps of approval. They were mere platforms leading to the next level, where he would gather another basket of golden eggs. Treasure waited ahead for whoever was plucky and energetic enough to grab it. Who says there are limits? If there are, a person won't know until he's thrown back totally exhausted for the third or fourth time.

As a result of these successes, early the next term he received an award from a local rehabilitation agency that he attended on off-school days. His picture and story in the college newspaper announced that James had been named "Patient of the Year" from among several hundred clients. That week I flagged down his wheelchair as he rocketed along a hallway. Reluctantly, he slowed so I could keep pace, consideration I rated as a professor. "Congratulations on your award," I said.

"For what?" he replied. "Pa-ti-ent of the Year? I am not a pa-ti-ent. Nor a cli-ent. I am a man." Then he pressed his hand down hard on the accelerator, pulled away from me toward a knot of shuffling students clogging the hallway, and shouted, "Com-ing through!"

M. GARRETT BAUMAN recently retired after many years as a professor and plans to write more about his students. He is a 2007–2008 fellow for The New York State Foundation for the Arts and has been published in _The Chronicle of Higher Education, Sierra, Yankee, The New York Times,_ and several issues of the Chrysalis Reader.

JACKIE BARTLEY

In April
the Bloodroot
Blossoms

They've found the bones of a fish
over three hundred million years old
poking from a fresh slice of Pennsylvania
roadcut. Rudiment of an upper arm bone
suggests it's a missing link between
animals who lived in water and those who first
ambled onto land.

                  Meanwhile, out in the stellar
sea, the space station crew circles home
listening to a strange drumming coming from
the instrument panel. Sound of flapping metal,
something broken, large or small, something
they hope they can fix without disaster.

Here, on solid ground, we limp along,
dodging the angry flak of words or bullets.
Spring comes in all its gaudy green pubescence.
Earth goes on curtsying, this way and that,
to the sun. It's like the game Pin the Tail
on the Donkey, all of us blindfolded, fumbling

toward something solid on which to attach
the blessings or sorrows we hold at arm's
length. Life is desire searching for a form.

JACKIE BARTLEY's work has appeared most recently in *Nimrod, Spillway,* and *Calyx.* Her latest collection, *Ordinary Time,* won the Spire Press Poetry Contest and was published in 2007. She lives with her husband and two crazed Dalmatians in Holland, Michigan.

Bringing the Past into the Future

NOT TOO LONG AFTER I started working as the editor at the Swedenborg Foundation, a manuscript arrived in my e-mail inbox. It wasn't a new book. It was the next stage in a project that had begun nearly twenty years ago: a guide to the writings of, and about, Emanuel Swedenborg (1688–1772), but it needed updating.

Who was Swedenborg? I thought. It's not an easy question to answer, and it was new to me. I discovered he was a scientist, a philosopher, an engineer, a scholar, a poet, a gentleman, and—more to the point for the countless people who have been inspired by his visions—a Christian mystic. Following a spiritual awakening in 1745, he devoted the remainder of his life to describing his journeys through heaven and hell and his conversations with angels and devils.

In a modern society it might be easy to dismiss Swedenborg's writings as delusion or a deliberate hoax. Even Swedenborg himself was aware of how unbelievable his reports sounded, and he was careful to draw as many examples as he could from society and nature to support what he wrote.

In the end, though, the most compelling proof of his writings is how consistently popular they've been. In the years following Swedenborg's death, his books influenced people like William Blake, Ralph Waldo Emerson, Immanuel Kant, Johann Wolfgang van Goethe, Henry David Thoreau, William Butler Yeats, Fyodor Dostoevsky, and Helen Keller (who loved Swedenborg's writings so much that she wrote a book of her own about them, *My Religion*).

There were thousands more who read Swedenborg over the years and, as the pages rolling out of my printer attested, they had a lot to say.

Anyone researching Western religious thought from the eighteenth century onward should include Swedenborg. His ideas, and his readers, show up in unusual places: for example, the first Swedenborgians in the U.S. arrived in Philadelphia shortly after the Revolutionary War and mingled with the founding fathers of our nation. At the same time that the transcendentalist movement was impacting art and literature, anti-slavery and women's rights activist Lydia Maria Child was reading Swedenborg and developing the personal convictions that drove her to "take on the establishment." At the turn of the twentieth century, a Swedenborgian minister helped to introduce Buddhism to the U.S.

With such a rich and varied history to work with, we probably shouldn't blame William Ross Woofenden for not wanting the job of sorting it all out. Although he first had the idea for the *Swedenborg Explorer's Guidebook* back in the 1960s, it took many years and much prodding from his colleagues to finally set it down on paper. It proved a difficult task. He took a sabbatical from his teaching position at the Swedenborg Theological Seminary to travel to Sweden, where Swedenborg was born and where many of Swedenborg's original manuscripts are still kept. Woofenden also visited the Swedenborg Society in London, which is a repository of rare editions and other Swedenborgian materials, as well as various sites around the U.S. Woofenden's first edition was published in 1988 under the title *Swedenborg Researcher's Manual,* to much applause from the Swedenborgian community.

In the two decades since the book was originally published, scholars have continued to make new discoveries about Swedenborg. In 2000, the Swedenborg Foundation launched a new series of translations of Swedenborg's writings to be called the New Century Edition. In 2002, a team of editors set to work updating Woofenden's original edition to include the latest developments. For me, reading the final result of their labor was a journey through the life and mind of Emanuel Swedenborg. Whatever you may think of what he wrote, he was undeniably a genius.

Although we're separated in time by two hundred and fifty years, Swedenborg speaks very well to our modern society. In America, there's a growing tension between religious fundamentalism and secular culture. With each passing year, it seems that the two sides have less to say to each other. One side insists that creationism be taught alongside science in schools; the other side dismisses creationism as myth. One side votes for leaders on the basis of how loudly they pro-

A banner—anchored by the author's office window on the third floor of the Swedenborg Foundation's 1773 building—says it all: old and new, a mutual celebration.

Published anonymously in 1758, *Heaven and Hell* is a detailed description of the afterlife, based on Emanuel Swedenborg's personal experiences. The book has remained in print for 250 years. Swedenborg's own copy may be seen today in Stockholm at the Swedish Royal Academy of Sciences, of which he was a long-time member.

claim their faith; the other seeks leaders who don't mention creation at all. One side promotes faith in God as the solution to a variety of social problems; the other side resents what it perceives as an attempt to force-feed faith.

Many people are caught in the middle of this conflict, seeking spiritual inspiration but not getting it from either their childhood churches or from charismatic evangelicals. Swedenborg was in much the same position; he was a man of faith but one whose religious ideas conflicted with the accepted teachings of the state church—so much so that he couldn't sell his own books in his native Sweden for fear of running afoul of church censorship. He was also a man of science, devoting much of his life to discovering how the world works and to furthering the knowledge of humankind. Some of his inventions, such as a flying machine and a submersible ship, were centuries ahead of his time. He understood science and religion as complementary, not mutually exclusive.

His visions of the afterlife were incredibly detailed and ultimately reassuring. God is a loving creator, he says, who does not punish or condemn humanity. It is human beings who decide their own fate. If they choose God's love and wisdom, they will find themselves doing good deeds and treating others well because they love it, and after death they will find themselves drawn into heaven. On the other hand, if people close themselves off to God and immerse themselves in selfish desires, after death they are repulsed by heaven, and of their own accord they go farther and farther away into hell.

Rather than rejecting this world, Swedenborg says, we should embrace it—not overindulging in physical pleasures, but not denying them either. His is the higher ground of engaging in the world around you, not judging others by the faith they proclaim (if they proclaim it at all) but by their actions and their intentions. In a dramatic departure from the religious teachings of the time, Swedenborg wrote that some non-Christians enter the heavenly world of spirit more directly than the Christians of his day, that a person can still be open to God even if he perceives God differently than Christians.* It's a message of tolerance that we need now as much as the people of his time needed it then.

When Swedenborg wrote about heaven and earth, he envisioned the coming of a new brotherhood of mankind, a world in which people approached faith, love, and charity in a completely different way than in the past. His writings are ultimately all about rebirth and renewal, and perhaps the greatest message we can take away from them is that it's never too late to start.

MORGAN BEARD is the editor at Swedenborg Foundation Publishers, a non-profit organization dedicated to producing works by and about Emanuel Swedenborg and educational materials and projects aimed at interesting people in Swedenborg. In her spare time, she teaches Japanese tea ceremony, writes fiction, and does research into Irish history and folklore. She lives just outside of Philadelphia with entirely too many cats.

---

* "non-Christians come into heaven more readily than Christians nowadays." . . . Christians do not live up to their doctrines as non-Christians do." *Heaven and Hell.* Paragraphs 324, 325, 326. (Swedenborg numbered the paragraphs in his works. In Swedenborgian studies it is customary to reference a particular text to the book's title and Swedenborg's paragraph number, as the numbers are uniform in all editions.)

Fieldwork

I FOUND MYSELF OUT OF SYNC, out of place, and out of time as I finished up my senior year of college. About to receive a degree in metallurgical engineering/materials science from Carnegie Mellon University (CMU), a top engineering school, I had bleak prospects. I had gone to job interviews with button-down-shirt-close-cropped-hair recruiters. Me—in my dirty bell bottoms, shoulder-length locks, thick beard, and earrings. This was 1972, and I was under the influence of the hippie culture. I knew I didn't fit in with U.S. Steel or Rockwell International. I felt like a Black Panther trying to join the Augusta National Golf Club.

At nearly the last minute, March of my senior year, I decided to apply to a number of graduate schools in metallurgical engineering/materials science. It was a long shot—I was about to graduate in two months *summa cum nada,* with an average eking into the two-point range, thanks only to my English and history courses. I had scored fairly well on my GRE, however, and my pedigree was CMU, and its metallurgical engineering department was ranked in the top three in the world.

After several rejection notices, the University of Cincinnati (UC) accepted me into their graduate program and saved me from a job I would have loathed, and likely, failed miserably. I should say that the University of Cincinnati put me in limbo. I spent the next two years treading water as a research assistant. As a lowly grad student, the university paid my tuition and a stipend, which was just enough to live on.

When I arrived in Cincinnati just five weeks after graduating, it took me about an hour to figure out why UC wanted a slug like me. I was American, spoke unaccented English, and had applied. The metallurgical engineering/materials science department was awash in research grants from the U.S. Defense Department and desperately needed dozens of graduate students to help conduct research for the profs rolling in the government's dough. I was one of six American graduate students in that department. The rest were Chinese and Indians, dozens of them. They were all extremely bright men—yes, all of them were men—and I befriended a number of them. But here's the point: many of them were from wealthy families in their native countries and worked in research labs for a lot less than my own stipend, and in some cases, for free. One young Indian grad student was so rich that he said he'd be insulted if the university paid him such a lowly amount of money. The American students all received living stipends, and the Ph.D. students received enough to afford car payments!

My lab mate was Yuann Kwang-lin, or Jimmy, for short. Jimmy was a native Taiwanese who desperately wanted me to help him learn English. He wanted to be able to pick up American girls, whom he perceived to be loose and available, unlike the few Chinese girls at hand. I helped him as best I could, his English improved markedly over the two years while we shared the lab, and he was eventually successful, which means that I was a successful teacher—my one success at the University of Cincinnati. As payment, I asked Jimmy to make a poster for me in Chinese characters that I could display in my lab space: "Take Heed. Screw You!" It took me weeks to convince this shy man to make such an impolite use of his native language. Last month, I finally discarded this poster, moldy and mildewed in my garage, after my eight-year-old son asked what it meant.

UC's engineering graduate students worked in laboratories. They ran experiments, collected data, gathered "findings," and wrote reports for the professors to send to the grantors, and eventually received master or doctorate degrees. We would work all day on our experiments, go home for dinner, and come back at night to the lab. At 9 PM, we left our labs and took up our table at the legendary Lakewood Bar across Colerain Avenue from the campus. Each night, seven nights a week, we drank and smoked cigarettes until 2 AM. This was in the 1970s, when you could smoke just about anywhere late into the morning—pitcher after pitcher, lighting butt-to-end chains, arguing over data, findings, and sports. . . . and girls—but for us graduate students, there were darn few of those to talk about.

During these two years, I lived only in the moment. I felt I had delayed my future, but I wasn't worried about that. I had no idea what my next step was, but it didn't occur to me to plan anything. I was floating on Little Kings Cream Ale, drifting on Marlboro smoke, and my research was failing miserably. My professor was a young Turk with a newly minted Ph.D. in materials science, which covers not only inert materials like plastics, but also biomedical materials. My young

Turk professor talked daily about his "friend at the National Science Foundation" who would award him his first research grant, as soon as I, his research student, acquired some good data.

I spent one year looking into a compound called hyaluronic acid, notable as being a component in the fluid of human joints. The theory was that this compound broke down, and its breakdown was critical in the development of arthritis. The compound was very difficult to isolate, and the hypothesis floating around at the time hoped to make hyaluronic acid synthetically, which would then somehow be used to treat arthritis, possibly as a replacement for the natural stuff in your knee. About the only thing I discovered in one year was that hyaluronic acid could not be isolated nor could it be made synthetically—at least not in my lab. After one year of frustration, my professor decided to drop that line of research and focused on coatings, i.e., paint, so that his "friend at the Sherwin-Williams company" could fund our research.

I spent the second year of my tenure at the University of Cincinnati developing various coating compounds, applying them to steel plates the size of index cards, and then soaking them in various solutions to track the corrosion resistance of the various coatings, and dropping weights on them to test the impact strength of the coatings. I spent several hundred dollars of my professor's personal money on large aquariums in which to soak the steel plates. I kept a few goldfish in them and one night, on a lark, tested the effects of liquid nitrogen on goldfish, actually flash freezing a goldfish and watching the little critter come back to life after I dropped it back into the room temperature water. I didn't tell my professor about that experiment. He had no friends in the cryogenics industry. About the only thing I truly accomplished in that second year was the development of this cool instrument that dropped weights on the metal plates from adjustable heights. A known weight dropped from a known height hits with a calculable force, and in that way I could detect the strength or resiliency of the coatings I had applied to the plates. Unfortunately, my results never seemed to be reproducible or consistent in any way. My methodologies were somehow not methodological, and I never did get the hang of designing the experiments correctly.

All of the other graduate students laughed at my efforts. After all, they were doing important research, like testing highly sophisticated titanium alloys used in jet engines. One of the students, Dane Miller, was testing materials for artificial joints, and after receiving his Ph.D., he founded Biomet, a hip- and knee-replacement manufacturer in Bloomington, Indiana, that reported sales of $1.6 billion in 2004. While Dane Miller's hip machine mimicked the stresses of years of walking by rubbing the ball of a stainless steel femur into a polyethylene cup for weeks and months, even while Dane was drinking beer at the Lakewood Bar, I was watching metal plates rust. My lack of data, my lack of clear "findings," spelled a lack of career progress for my professor. My research was literally worthless, and at the end of two years, I had only one clear finding: I was not going to receive a master's degree.

It was during this time that I started writing a lot: fiction, poetry, nonfiction. It was the one thing I was good at in college, and to amuse myself, I spent time writing short stories, weird poems, and kept a journal. This was also the Watergate era, and the stories of Woodward and Bernstein permeated the air. I would often stay at home from the lab, mesmerized by the televised Watergate hearings. Because I was a tuition-free graduate student, I was allowed to take courses anywhere in the university, so I took a few courses in journalism during my two years at UC. The university did not have a journalism department, but there was a track of three journalism courses in the English department, taught by a young prof named Jon Hughes, a former reporter. I mastered "the 5 W's" and the "inverted pyramid," but most importantly, got to know Professor Hughes because we tipped a few mugs together, and he shared his stories from daily newsroom work. I expressed my desire to get out of engineering and possibly into journalism. He suggested that I write a sample article or two for a small local biweekly newspaper, *The Clifton-Vine Reporter*, which covered five urban neighborhoods within the city, all of which surrounded the university area. I lived in one of those neighborhoods, called Clifton, just off the corner of Clifton and Ludlow Avenues, a block from the Virginia Bakery and the Skyline Chili parlor. The idea for beginning journalists is to acquire what is known in the trade as "clips," or samples of published work to build a resumé. Jon told me that he would speak with the editor of the paper about me. This was in the summer of 1974, Watergate in full swing.

A couple of beers later with Jon Hughes, he mentioned that the editor of that little newspaper would interview me and asked if I'd be interested in meeting him. I jumped at the chance. The next afternoon I walked into the offices of Richard Bird, who was one of the more unusual characters I've met. The man had the worst case of blue-black acne I'd ever seen, even on the face of a teenager, and he was clearly in his thirties. He smelled foul, like not showering in days, and his face was oily and shiny, his clothing disheveled and dirty. Ben Bradlee, he was not. He interviewed me for fifteen minutes, then gave me my first assignment. I was to cover the next day's City Council meeting and write an article about an issue of concern to his audience—the elimination of gas lights on the streets of these old neighborhoods. I attended the council meeting the following day, made a few follow-up phone calls, wrote the piece, and handed it to Mr. Bird.

My first article was published in the following issue of this biweekly newspaper. Mr. Bird took me out for a beer that night. I was quite naïve back then, and, remember, this was the 1970s when things were not as open then as they are now. While I noticed that the bar was filled only with men, some dressed as cowboys, right in the middle of the city, it didn't register as it might today. Mr. Bird seemed nervous, asking several personal questions, but I was quite confident about my writing and riveted upon his every word. He was my new boss. I was open to his tutelage, and he held the keys to a new path for me. He told some war stories about his reporting, about his connections at City Hall, about the history of *The Clifton-Vine Reporter,* and about the typographics company he ran alongside it, which supported the paper financially. Then he asked: "Do you want to become editor of this newspaper?" Bird said that he needed to step back from the hands-on effort and work more on the business side of the operation. I was dumbstruck, but not struck dumb. Of course I jumped at the opportunity. I became the editor-in-chief of this little newspaper, my first job. The pay, $100 per issue, biweekly, meant $200 per month. I would have to give up my research stipend, which was more than double that amount.

The day before Thanksgiving 1974, I walked into my professor's office and told him that I was leaving engineering to become a journalist. He told me I was crazy, and so did my father, when I told him on a visit home that holiday weekend. But I felt that I had thrown away six years of my life, four to get a B.S. in engineering that I would never use and two more years failing to get a graduate degree. I knew in my gut that I was beginning something that I wanted to do, that I loved to do, that I was built for. I had a sense of purpose . . . I felt it physically, inside. My direction felt right for the first time in years.

About two months after I started at the *Clifton-Vine Reporter,* Mr. Bird departed abruptly when an audit of the business uncovered his hand in the till. I never saw him again. I spent the next two years at that little biweekly newspaper, and that's where I learned journalism, made some mistakes, did more things right, and had fun. I wrote many of the articles. I pasted up the newspaper by hand (this is before desktop publishing). I delivered the proofs to the printer and then delivered the newspapers to the horde of ten-year-olds who delivered the papers to the doors of five neighborhoods in Cincinnati. I hired a couple of reporters, for $10 a story. I hired two reviewers, one for books and one for music, and that music reviewer, Steven Rosen, later became a top music critic at the *Cincinnati Enquirer* and the *Denver Post.* After that, I landed a job on a small daily, the

A.R. Penck.
Eau de Cologne.
Synthetic polymer
paint on canvas,
114¼ in. x 114¼ in.,
1975. The Museum of
Modern Art, New York.
Anne and Sid Bass Fund.
Digital image ©The
Museum of Modern
Art/Licensed by SCALA /
Art Resource, New York.
©A. R. Penck, 2008.

Middletown Journal, then went on to earn an M.S. in journalism at Ohio University. In 1978, I finally used my engineering degree when I landed a job at *IEEE Spectrum,* a science and engineering magazine in New York City, which won the first of its three national magazine awards while I worked there. I covered the first space shuttle launch and the Three Mile Island nuclear accident while on staff there.

Wanting to leave New York City and sensing opportunity at a small publishing company in Tennessee, I relocated to Knoxville in 1982, to work for the firm that eventually became fast-growing and innovative Whittle Communications. I grew with it, rising to executive editor, running a large group of media properties and a staff of twenty-five editors and designers. During those years, I became an expert in health and medical media. During my time in Knoxville, I lost a wife and remarried. In 1994, I moved to Portland, Oregon, where I helped start up the first commercial health website, then was recruited to Atlanta in 1998 to help start up the firm that eventually became the Internet juggernaut WebMD. I was, and still am, the founding editor-in-chief of WebMD, leaving there in 2001 to go back to my first love, creative writing. I've since earned an MFA in creative writing from the Queens University of Charlotte, have published numerous poems, essays, and criticism, one chapbook of poems, and, ever-still an editor, have just published an anthology of poems that I compiled.

Mr. Bird, the man who handed me my first job in journalism, unfortunately, met a tragic end. Jon Hughes, now a retired professor, told me the story during one of our periodic phone calls. He was murdered by a young man he had picked up in a bar, after a tryst in his apartment. The man stabbed him to death, and then apparently became so panicked by what he had done that he fled through the window and ran right off the second story roof, breaking his leg in the fall, allowing him to be captured by police.

I often wonder what Mr. Bird saw in me.

TOM LOMBARDO's poems have appeared or are forthcoming in the U.S., U.K., Canada, and India in *Oxford American, Ambit, Subtropics, Southern Poetry Review, Pearl, New York Quarterly, Poet Lore, Asheville Poetry Review, Orbis: Quarterly International Literary Journal, Hampden-Sydney Poetry Review, Salamander, Kritya: A Journal of Poetry, The Louisville Review, Hawai'i Review, Crucible, The Worcester Review, Ascent, Ars Medica,* and many others. His literary criticism has appeared in *New Letters, North Carolina Literary Review,* and *South Carolina Review.* His nonfiction has appeared in *IEEE Spectrum, Leisure* magazine, and most recently in Chrysalis Reader. An anthology that he's edited—*After Shocks: The Poetry of Recovery for Life-Shattering Events* (Sante Lucia Books)—will be released Autumn 2008 (www.poetryofrecovery.com). In addition to his poetry and nonfiction writing, he is a medical and health editor, and he was the founding editor-in-chief of the website WebMD.com. He lives in midtown Atlanta and has taught courses in creative writing and in aesthetics at the Atlanta College of Art.

First Lessons

Spindle-stacked symphonies,
up to a half dozen brittle 78s,
tumbling one after the other
onto the old RCA turntable.
Music, always, infusing
crevices and dusty corners.

Pre-pubescent, I knew nothing
of orgasmic shudders the first time
I heard Casals—Vivaldi's Concerto for Cello.
Inchoate stirrings welled up unbidden,
goose-bumped, shivers
up and down the spine, a flushing
warmth coursing veins,
a glistening in the eyes—ecstasy,
bliss unfamiliar words.

Richer than fresh cream
smoother than a fine Port
deeper than the deepest well—ah, the elegance!
Of a sudden life seemed so simple—
I wanted nothing more
than to replicate that sound
with my own two hands.

        A loaner cello,

Homeward, arms gentle around it
caressing it as a lover would. Cradled
between my knees, a cautious drawing

of the bow across catgut and steel and, oh God!,
the sound! Worse than alley cats
caterwauling at midnight.

                And so to first lessons
the drudgery of scales, arpeggios
the incitement of war between
impetuosity and patience. "Young man,"
she said, "you will never know the possibilities
until you can play with your eyes closed."

Although his education and vocation have been otherwise directed, KRIKOR
DER HOHANNESIAN has been writing poetry for the past thirty-five years—
writing being his first love. His work has appeared most recently in *The
Evansville Review, The South Carolina Review, Sulphur River Literary Review,
The New Renaissance,* and *Permafrost.* Krikor comes from a family of artists,
writers, and musicians and is a graduate of Harvard University. Now semi-
retired, he can direct more energy at long last to writing. He also serves as
assistant treasurer of the New England Poetry Club.

How Does It Begin?

WHEN I RETURNED HOME FROM THE MEMORIAL SERVICE for my *shakuhachi* (Japanese bamboo flute) teacher, Masakazu Yoshizawa, and thought of the papers I still had to grade, I did not sit down to mark up essays with that pedantic pen that tells the bewildered student: if you correct this paper, you'll correct your life. Instead, although dazed and exhausted, I entered my practice room to play my flute, listen to what sounds were stirring inside me, now that the man who taught me how to make those sounds was gone. While warming up, I thought of Rumi's "The Reed Flute's Song":

> Listen to the story told by the reed,
> of being separated.

> "Since I was cut from the reedbed,
> I have made this crying sound.

> Anyone apart from someone he loves
> understands what I say.

> Anyone pulled from a source
> longs to go back."

In a sense, I felt "pulled from a source," the reedbed that was my teacher, and all I could hear now was "this crying sound." But at the same time, the notes were connecting me to him, and so I played "Tamuke," a *honkyoku* (a meditation piece) to help the dead cross over. And though I have played this piece throughout my seventeen years of lessons with Masa, never before had I heard the grief, the tonal vibrato in the notes. Rumi says, "The reed is hurt and salve com-

Carol Lem

Shinoda Tôkô.
Sprout D.
Lithograph,
ink and color on paper,
23½ x 17¾ in.,
Shôwa period.
Harvard University Art
Museums, Arthur M.
Sackler Museum.
Gift of Art/Asia Gallery.
Photograph by Imaging
Department
©President and Fellows
of Harvard College.

bining. Intimacy and longing for intimacy, one song." And I wanted to stay where I was—inside such a pure, hollow note, be nourished and renewed by it everyday. Rumi speaks of "the secrets hidden within the notes," how the body flows out of spirit, spirit out of body. Is this the secret, I wonder, or the mystery of the secret—that nameless *something* as though another were with you in the room, this something, this "crying sound" that is both empty and regenerative? The Japanese say that you cannot fill your teacup unless you empty it. And so, too, this Persian mystic poet reminds me that poetry and music are possible only because we're empty, hollow, "pulled from a source," and long to return. Is creating language and music, then, a longing for home, a longing to go back to the source that renews the spirit? As a teacher, Masa helped me to do that, but now more than ever his teachings would instill in me the reedbed of creation, the simple act of making something.

Sitting with a friend over a bowl of noodles at a small café in Little Tokyo after the service, she asked if I had been doing any writing since that's been my usual morning routine. "No," I said, "been too overwhelmed catching up with essay grading, but tomorrow I will." So as I sat in my practice room, weaving in and out of thoughts of my teacher's passing, yet thinking how beautiful the morning is, along with the sweet, pure soprano voice of Margaret Price singing the closing aria of Vaughan Williams' *Pastoral Symphony*, I followed the words to see where they would take me as I sorted out the stimuli and attempted to discover the hidden secrets of the reedbed.

Like the aria, I find as Eliot does, "in my end is my beginning," that the solo song I must make for myself is a renewal not only of spirit but of all those beginning lessons I learned from my teacher and recorded on discs. For when I listen to them now, it is with the knowledge that he will not be there Saturday (the usual day for my lesson) to correct my pitch, intonation, and rhythm; I have only the voice and sounds on the recording to replay over and over until my listening reaches a more deep and profound level as though I were hearing it all for the very first time. It is this music of instruction that I was thinking of while writing "The Music Goes On":

Waking to a light veil of haze
glazing the canyon hills, a sea of clouds beyond
as in a Japanese landscape

I hear your flute still,
your long sustained note, alive as this hour
when time falls back

and you are sitting beside me
showing me how to lift from my lap
the *shakuhachi*, graceful as a Zen practitioner

before an altar, how to place
the embrasure to my lips, and with that first
intake of air blow gently out.

For then you are ready, you said,
ready as the morning is ready to renew itself
with each sound and breath

as it enters the trees and sky,
every passerby who hears me play *Korogi Tsukiyo*,
Cricket in Moonlight, tonight

on my balcony when night song and morning song
survive in the memories of our playing
side by side

in your living room on Kimdale
where we sat before a mantel of photographs
and instruments, wind chimes, and singing bowl

that echoes now like a temple bell
calling us home
while the music goes on.

The secret of this readiness for renewal, I am rediscovering, is entered through listening to "each sound and breath." This listening became so evident to me when Masa and I collaborated on a CD, a reading of selected poems from my book, *Shadow of the Plum*, with his music. The title, *Shadow of the Bamboo*, a duet of poetry and music, was decided on for I felt that my reading, his playing, compositions and arrangements were not just an accompaniment to a reading but a *duet*, two musical entities—alone but together—communing to create a third presence. I remember the morning I arrived at his house in San Gabriel: the living room was dim as usual, microphone and chair set up for me, and his recording equipment carefully arranged on the floor. I had assumed he was going to play as I read but instead he said, "Let's test your voice in the mike," and as he fiddled with knobs, moving levers up and down like a technician in the sound booth, I arranged my poems in the order I was to read them. Later while alone, he listened to my recorded poems and composed the diverse themes like a soundtrack to a film.

During the next few days, he would call me asking about a poem, such as who was the "you" in this room. Though Masa's conversational English was pretty good, this project demanded not only his skills in applying his second language but his interpretive skills in translating literary text, which involved *listening* to tones, nuances, the various shades of meaning, in order for his music and my words to become one. When he told me he had to read the poems and listen to my prerecorded voice repeatedly to get sense and meaning right for the musical themes and sound effects, I imagined us having late night conversations though each was in our solitary workplace.

Two weeks later when I heard the individual tracks, carefully composed to bring out the story and ambience of each poem, I felt three of us there. Though I had written the poems alone and he had composed late into early morning alone, we were together, two spirits renewed by the third, the creation of our collaboration.

Collaboration

Begins with you taking the clarinet
from your black case, assembling the parts,
attaching the reed,

Stravinsky's *Three Pieces*
spread on the table. It begins with listening
to the haunting moody strains,
the words to a poem clicking like ice
in two glasses of tea.

A few written lines . . . and then
your shakuhachi blows past the block
in my muse's heart

to the opening of *Duet,* "Your sweet bamboo
should come first, I say, not verse."

And you imagine now . . .
the score of an unfinished story.

But whose story? Mine, yours—or
this other, this meeting between us with a pen
and flute composing a different silence,

the kind where the image fades into music
rising in that measured space, *Ma,* Japanese call it,
and disappearing into a momentary stillness,
more felt than heard

but impossible without the words, the notes,
this sixth sense, you say,
                              this *other*
we are giving voice to
today.

It wonders who the "you" is "crossing the lawn
toward me / with a red rose," lines
from long ago flowing through the bamboo flute
like a displaced spirit.

When I say it's a man, not a woman, you hear
a door open as though someone
                              has come through,
the tone drops a pitch.
You say, "I understand"

and add your own inflection of lost love
now that the image is yours
and this other meeting between us.

From endings come beginnings, especially after the passing of someone or something dear to you—a parent, soul mate, spouse, even a pet. Suddenly, you find yourself in solitude either welcomed or imposed. Like May Sarton and so many who depend on the tools of release and re-creation, I know the value of solitude, and "one of its values," she says, "is, of course, that there is nothing to *cushion against attacks from within* . . . ." So you pick up a pen or musical instrument to give shape to that attack within. Out of this sensibility came, "Though You Are Gone."

The sound, the breath
of bamboo groves, leaves the body
for our posterity, new cells
and vessels, estuaries
to the rivers of our soul,
to say death too flows along
the watercourse way and air waves,
filling the flute
with fresh tones, deep and pure
as underground springs

while spirit fills the diaphragm,
eases up and out through the open gate
of the throat first sounds, *Ajikan,*
the Japanese say and the shakuhachi player
knows while she sits zazen
from hour to hour, traveling
the uncertain passages of diminuendo
and crescendo, for the mapmaker
is gone.

But we have your teachings
to explore like undiscovered treasure
embedded in the sea floor
of heart and mind, for didn't
you say the fingers remember,
listen to them and not the scribbled notes
on the page, they are just memos
for the music within.

Pitch tone to the spheres, you said,
harmonize with the stars;
but now as you *are* a tone
in an unnamed constellation,
my daily practice reaches for that other
dimension where as teacher
and student, I am still
striving to match my sound
with yours.

Now when I enter the practice room, it is with this sense of renewal—by *listening* to his sounds, the resonating shades of nuances,
as he so closely *listened* to my words. For it begins with that first light
of healing as strongly felt as the sun blazing through the window like
rays of healing after weeks of wind-swept rains, and the music is just
right while the white, blank page waits to fill. It is that moment of
crossing over between the dreamy state of nothingness, before the
world has entered, and that impulse to write first words, rising from
the bombardment of stimuli that life hands us to sort out. I often
wonder what people do who don't write or play an instrument, or
paint—these tools of release and re-creation. Renewal begins with
that first word, first sound, that opening stroke, as in a Japanese
painting when a bird is born. By staying open to the journey that first
words, first sounds take me on, I will write and play my way back to
the source, the reedbed, home. Zen practitioners speak of the importance of having a spiritual practice. Mine continues to be the pen and
the *shakuhachi.*

CAROL LEM lives in Sierra Madre, California, and teaches literature and creative writing at East Los Angeles College. She has been writing poetry and
playing the shakuhachi since the 1960s. Her work has recently been published in *Blue Arc West, an Anthology of California Poets; Living in Storms,
Contemporary Poetry and the Moods of Manic Depression; Hawaii Pacific
Review, Best of the Decade 1997–2007,* and *Writers at Work, Poem of the
Month (March 2008)* online series. A reading of selected poems from her
current book, *Shadow of the Plum,* may be heard on her CD, *Shadow of the
Bamboo,* with music by Masakazu Yoshizawa. For an excerpt of this CD, vis-
it www.carollem.com.

Kelly for a Day

Purse.
Silk, gold, silver, linen,
5½ in. (height),
British, last quarter
sixteenth century.
The Metropolitan
Museum of Art, New
York. Purchase, Judith
and Gerson Leiber Fund,
1986. Image
©The Metropolitan
Museum of Art.

I WAS MOVING FROM SAN FRANCISCO TO SEATTLE and decided I wanted to bring with me a new name. I didn't want a name like Sunshine or Moonbeam. I was leaving my hippie life in California and moving on to serious business.

For some time I had been studying the Tarot with a professional reader, whose name was Nirvana, and it was she who had emphasized the benefits of a changed name. "It's a positive affirmation," she said, and she was earning sixty dollars for her readings. Her original name had been Peggy Swartzler, and she told me more than once how changing her name had changed her life. "I just can't hear the name Peggy without remembering being a fat person," she'd said, running her hand down her slim hip.

One of my friends had gone from *Darlene* to *Asia*, and another from *Janice* to *Persia*, and there didn't seem to be too many interesting countries left. *China* did have a nice sound, but my grandmother had always said, ominously, while discussing world situations: "People focus on Russia, but it's China we need to keep our eye on!"

Finally, it happened my last day in California. The need for a new name was causing me to feel a lot of pressure. That morning I decided that the first name I saw that day that I liked, or at least could tolerate, would be the name that the Universe intended for me to have. *All I have to do is walk around and wait for it to come,* I concluded.

With that settled, I went downstairs to get the mail for the last time and discovered my neighbor's telephone bill in my box. Her name was Vera Kelly. *Ahh,* I thought, and it was like a flash, *Kelly Campbell will be my new name!* I had hoped for something more spiritual or esoteric, and *Kelly* seemed a little too cute, but I was exhausted from the whole idea.

I could hardly wait to really *be* Kelly Campbell, and my mind began designing business cards I would have printed for the new Tarot reader in town. I had had my ticket for over a week, and several times a day I would get it out from the inside pocket of my purple velvet cape and stare at the airplane soaring above the clouds on the envelope.

The afternoon passed slowly while I sat and dreamed of my new life. Finally, it was early evening, and there was one more thing left to do. On 24th Avenue was a metaphysical bookstore with a sign in the window: "Psychic Readings: An evening with St. Ives." I had planned to have a reading there on my last day in California, so I could digest on the plane the next morning all the wonderful things that I was sure the psychic would tell me.

I took off my jeans and T shirt and dressed in my gypsy costume, a long wraparound dress with splashes of color. I was pleased to notice that one of the main colors in the dress was green—*kelly* green. That seemed like a real omen, I decided. Then I added my long, brass earrings from India, my Egyptian bracelets, and I was ready to leave, wearing what I called my business suit.

I began walking up Valencia Street on my way to the bookstore, listening to my earrings hum as they bounced against my cheeks. My bracelets tingled as they rolled up and down my arms, and the sound was strangely exhilarating.

I entered the store and walked past the astrology books, gazing at them longingly. I glanced at the display of Tarot cards from various countries and cultures, and stopped to smell the burning incense. Sitar music was playing softly. There were quartz and crystals on counters and shelves, and stones of various sizes and colors. "All the tools of my trade," I thought. I lingered at the counter and asked to see a turquoise and coral necklace that was behind glass. The price was higher than I'd paid for my airplane ticket, but I held it for a minute, absorbing the Aquarian Age vibrations.

I headed for the back room where the readings were held, with my beaded velvet handbag, where my personal Tarot cards were kept, swinging lightly against my hip. The room was small and full of people sitting on folded chairs, laughing and chattering. It was obvious they knew each other and had been here before. I found a chair and sat down quietly—the only serious person in the bunch.

A door opened, and a stooped and elderly black man entered wearing a faded blue work shirt and khaki pants that were slightly too large. He introduced himself as Joe or Jim, and his voice had a heavy Mississippi or Alabama accent. I was disappointed and wondered briefly if it might be possible to get my money back.

Instantly the room was silent, and everyone faced the elderly man. Their backs became straight and hands were folded in laps. The man appeared to go to sleep. His head fell forward, and he was almost snoring. The room remained silent, except for the breathing, which appeared to be getting deeper and further away.

I felt restless and squirmed a little in my chair. The chair began to squeak, and I stopped instantly. *What kind of gyp joint is this?* I wondered. I'd been to plenty of readings with crystal balls and candles and bells and cards, but never with a little old man in a wrinkled shirt who went to sleep.

Time seemed to stop, and it was hard for me not to continue squirming. I looked at the barren walls, wishing there were some of those posters from India of the deities with all the arms, or the photograph of President Nixon with the caption: "Would you buy a used car from this man?"

Then the door opened again, and the owner of the store stepped in. He was wearing a white madras shirt and some kind of yogi pants, which made me feel better. He was smiling, probably at the size of the crowd. He greeted several people by name and welcomed us all to an evening with St. Ives, while the elderly black man continued to snore. Then he wrapped a blue bandanna around the sleeping man's head.

He walked down the aisles, passing out small yellow pencils, like the kind in the welfare office, and slips of paper. We were instructed to write one question on our paper and not to sign our name. *This would have been a good chance to use my new name,* I thought, as I wrote down the one question I had been planning to ask: "Will I be a successful Tarot reader in Seattle?" I was already sure I would be, and so was my teacher, but it would be interesting to actually hear the words from . . . I glanced at the sleeping reader again and felt my enthusiasm begin to wane. Then a basket was passed, and we dropped our folded questions inside.

When the basket was placed in front of the sleeping old man, to my surprise, he instantly reached inside and removed one of the questions. His body jerked, his head shot straight up, and a booming voice filled the room. There wasn't a trace of a southern accent, and his enunciation of every word was loud and clear. I'd heard the expression: "The hairs stood up on the back of my neck," and I wondered if this was happening to me. I couldn't remember when I'd felt more alert.

As various slips of paper were haphazardly chosen from the basket, he answered each question in that same strong voice. A little voice in my head kept wondering if there were holes in his bandanna. Ahhs and sighs were emitted around me, along with knowing glances and eyes meeting eyes. *Wait 'til they hear about me,* I thought. *This reading would have been a good place to drum up some business for myself!* I reached down and patted my Tarot cards, which were always with me.

A young girl was sitting next to me, wearing a tight-fitting tank top showing her cleavage. She leaned forward as the voice boomed her question: "Does my boyfriend really love me, or is he just saying so?" Her name was spoken, and I wondered if she'd written her name on the paper. I wondered if the psychic had seen it through the holes in his bandanna.

The answer was ambivalent, and the young girl appeared to be disappointed. "Meeting you again tonight," the voice continued, "has brought back marvelous memories of the earth plane." Everyone laughed. I was glad I hadn't written down the question that had been my second choice: "Will I meet my soul mate in Seattle?"

Then the voice began to chuckle. "And we have someone here tonight, for the first time, who has just begun to call herself Kelly." The voice chuckled again, and a few people joined in. "She asks if she will be a successful Tarot reader in Seattle."

The voice was quiet for a minute. Gently it answered: "No, I don't see you being a Tarot reader in Seattle. I don't see that as your path."

I was stunned, and my first thought was *There goes the name Kelly.* Then I remembered that I hadn't written the name on the paper nor had I told anyone *Kelly* would be my Seattle name. I stared at my hands and at the little velvet purse containing my shiny new Tarot cards. The voice continued: "If you keep a journal, pay attention to your dreams and spend time near water, your path will be revealed."

I walked out with mixed feelings, leaving the name *Kelly* at the door.

LORAINE CAMPBELL is a survivor of "The Summer of Love" in the late sixties in San Francisco. Her poems and short stories have appeared in *Grit, The Sun, Tacenda, Mother Earth, Chiron Review, Sounds of a Gray Metal Day, St. Linus Review, Wild Violet, Her Mark, Thorny Locust,* The Chrysalis Reader, and other serial publications. Some of this work also became pamphlets. She is working on a chapbook, "Squirm."

Finishing

His hands, blue-veined and wrinkled,
glide over the wood, like boats
sailing deep waters, sensing
the grain's heft and wallow.
He pauses now and then
to reread a portion of the story
embedded in the ancient walnut
then moves on, fingertips
touching the wood like calipers
measuring the depth and thickness
to a precision beyond physics,
beyond the actual, not looking
so much as drifting into the wood,
eyes closed, as if to enter
the grain on his own terms,
no distraction, no impediment,
striving to reach an understanding
between wood and worker,
between mind and matter.
He bends down close
to blow over the grain,
to clear away the surface
like God breathing life into clay,
then touches once more until
satisfied there is nothing more
he can do to alter the finish,
the inevitable feel of old wood
manicured to a tactile state
as if the grain contains
the old man himself,
his patience, his heart.

FRANK JAMISON writes poetry and fiction in Roane County, Tennessee. His first book of poetry, *Marginal Notes,* was published in 2001. His work has appeared in numerous journals. He received the Robert Burns Award of Excellence from the Knoxville Writers' Guild and won the 2005 Libba Moore Gray Poetry Award. He was nominated in 2006 for a Pushcart Prize.

Ribbons
of Lavender

IN THE CAR, MY MOTHER CROUCHED FORWARD, her hands glued to the wheel, her eyes pinned to the road. It drove me so crazy I wanted to roll down the window and yell. I was overtired from babysitting last night, and I loved Jimmy Gifford, but he stopped giving me any attention. Screaming wouldn't help make me feel better, so I said nothing.

There we were, as usual—my mother holding on and me holding back. Our biggest problem was that we missed my dad. Back in April he had a heart attack and died, just two months short of my graduation. My mother has been lost ever since, and I've been trying to keep her going.

This morning, my mother had to meet with her lawyer; something about reviewing a couple of documents for probate. They needed to discuss my father's assets, as if he had any. Other than the usual stuff—a car, house, furniture, and a small savings account—there was nothing. To make things worse, some sort of a snag prevented my mother from receiving ownership of the house and car. Her name wasn't listed on all the documents, so it would take longer to pass through the court.

I offered to go with her, but she said it was more important that I went to work and saved for college. That made me feel worse, as though I'd never have enough for even a community college.

My mother parked the car in back of the hotel. She leaned over and kissed my cheek. "Have a nice day, dear."

"You too," I mumbled, but the sky didn't seem any brighter.

Inside the housekeeping office, Mrs. Condon barked orders at me. "Okay, Miss O'Neill, you have the last wing."

Great! More linen to bring and further to push my cart.

"And I expect all sixteen rooms to be completed by one-thirty."
Truly my lucky day!

A maid could be assigned up to sixteen rooms. A veteran like Toni Miles got half the workload, but my friend Jill and I usually got punished with all sixteen.

Last week I thought about leaving this dump and finding a job elsewhere. This torture certainly drove home my point. Only I kept returning, day after day. What other summer job could I find?

"Good morning, Mrs. Condon."

I didn't have to turn around to see who had arrived. The sugary voice, the pretentious charm. A former chambermaid, Barbara Doyle, now served as the restaurant hostess. She obviously wanted something from me as she always did whenever she associated with us peons.

"I love your hair, Mrs. Condon."

"Thank you, Barbara. How was your day off?"

"Super! Jimmy Gifford and I had a wonderful time." Her voice directed at me.

I had to leave the room.

Loading up my cart, I wondered what Jimmy saw in someone like her. A lot, I supposed. She was perfect, a real Barbie doll. Blue eyes that sparkled, bleached white teeth that dazzled, blonde hair that curled just enough on the ends to highlight her shoulders, an incredible figure with long legs and slim hips. Any girl at my high school would have to stuff her bra to mirror Barbara's chest.

I knocked on the door with 114 printed on it. "Housekeeping," I announced, repeating the warning, then knocking again. No answer. Slowly, I opened the door, turned on the lights, and found the room vacant.

In a circular sweep, I dusted the furniture, then changed the bed. The occupant left the room in good condition. Most guests didn't. I switched on the bathroom light, took out the rag from my pocket, and cleaned the sink. Then I washed the counter and sanitized the toilet—I absolutely hated that word *sanitized*. It sounded as if I was restoring sanity to the thing. I pushed back the shower curtain and scrubbed the bathtub.

I deduced an airline pilot stayed here. Pilots never left messes, and they even left seat covers down. Either they had good training or their contracts stipulated they'd be fired if they weren't neat.

Room 116 required more work. I changed two beds and scrubbed the sink and chrome to remove the dried toothpaste stuck to them. A messy child must have stayed here.

Opposite:
Arnaldo Pomodoro
Traveler's Column.
Polished bronze,
103 in. (height),
1960–1965. Saint Louis
Art Museum.
Museum purchase.

Room 115 resembled the aftermath of a hurricane. Two beds and a cot had to be changed. Blankets and sheets were strewn about the room. Empty beer bottles cluttered the dresser and the table. Underneath the bottles sticky, clear rings glared up at me. Dried soap marks clouded the mirror. Towels littered the bathtub. As I started to collect them, I discovered they were sopping wet and smelled of old throw up. An inch or two of water still coated the tub. I had to wring out the towels before lugging them into the hallway and disinfecting the whole bathroom.

Perfectly programmed to knock and announce my entry, I dragged myself over to 110. I prayed that maybe the room was unoccupied and by mistake Condon had assigned it to me.

How glorious I would feel being on the receiving end. Just once. Oh to be a guest in a hotel, propped up in bed as a maid came in to dust, straighten up, and clean the bathroom. Only I'd leave the bathroom spotless, so no one would have to *sanitize* it.

Going to another movie with Jimmy wouldn't be so bad either. Not having my mother work so hard would be even better. Having my father back would be the best. But who was I kidding? My life was a chain of mishap after mishap, tied tightly around my neck like a dog collar.

If only one person would be nice to me, empathize with my suffering, and say they were sorry. Then I'd accept my misery. Feel understood.

I repeated my "Housekeeping" announcement, then opened the 110 door with clean linen in my hands.

My back throbbed as I stripped the bed. A massage would suit me fine.

"Get to work or I'll send you home!" Imitating Condon's growl, Jill peered inside my room. Instead of going for a cigarette, she visited me, providing comic relief whenever she could get away with it.

"What time did you get here?" I asked, unfurling the top sheet.

"Shortly after seven," Jill answered, grabbing hold of one side of the sheet. "I'm only taking a five-minute break. Maybe I'll impress Condon, and she'll let me leave early."

Jill's sister was baptizing the twins today. We had bets on whether she'd be allowed to go home early, despite Condon's promise from last week.

"Good luck," I said, the doubt thick in my voice.

After helping me with the bedspread, Jill panned the room. "Condon always gives you the messiest."

"Yeah, second in a row. This one must have been a nervous wreck. A female. There's dried nail polish by the phone, and the sheets were a crumbled mess."

"Good deduction, Sherlock." Jill leaned against the bureau. "How was baby-sitting last night?"

"Terrific! This time Mrs. Michaelson was four hours late." I rolled up the dirty sheets in a ball and flung them onto the pile in the hall-way.

"That's awful!"

"And this morning I had to hear the latest Jimmy-loves-Barbie episode."

Jill waved down her arm. "Hey, you're too good for him anyway."

"Thanks."

I savored my dates with Jimmy—to the movies, to our high-school basketball games. He even went with me to my mother's craft show. Then one day Barbie appeared on the scene. Jimmy was pick-ing me up from work. He waited in the parking lot. By the time I walked out the door, Barbie had already strolled into his life.

Under the hood of her Camaro, Jimmy had jiggled various hoses and asked her to start the car. The engine turned over immediately. Barbie popped out of the car and smacked a kiss on his cheek, her breasts flattening against Jimmy's chest. I was nauseated.

"Ready to go, Jimmy?" I asked although I knew it was already too late.

Jimmy turned around. "Be right with you," his annoyance blatant in his scowl.

Wiggling back to her car, Barbie flashed him a smile, then got into the driver's seat.

Watching her pull away, Jimmy asked, "What's her name?"

"Barbara Doyle," I said, rolling my eyes. "She goes to Avon High."

"Why didn't you introduce me before?"

"You weren't wearing any garlic around your neck. But then again, that wouldn't have protected you from her vampire bite."

After that day, the two of them went steady. Every time I saw Jimmy in school or in the parking lot at the hotel, he walked past me as if I didn't even exist.

Jill smiled to cheer me up. "Cindy, there are other fish in the sea."

I looked around the room. "Where?"

"Well, maybe not here—"

"Thanks, but I'm still stuck on you-know-who."

"Well, you need to get unstuck. In the meantime, I should get back to the dungeon—I mean my next room." She headed out the door.

"Good luck with leaving early."

"I'll let you know what Condon says."

For some reason, Jill's words stuck in my head: *Other fish in the sea.* Jimmy and I dated months ago. If I got out more, maybe I'd get over him.

Jill offered to set me up with her cousin several times. He was a year younger than we were, a junior at Cheney Tech. I should have said yes and forgotten that I ever pledged my undying love to Jimmy, but some things were easier to think about than do.

If I stayed home all the time, I'd end up like my mother. I knew she was grieving for my father, and that it would take time for her to put her life back together and start going places again other than church or work or the grocery store. She never went out to a movie or to dinner with a friend, not even a girlfriend.

A maid sign hung on the doorknob of room 108. I knocked, then heard a female voice say, "Come in."

I unlocked the door and spotted an old black woman sitting at the table by the window. She wore a lavender bathrobe that fit tightly around her middle. Her hair sat on her head in thick, gray coils. She read from a book. Judging from the red edging and the ribbon markers, I figured it was a Bible.

"Would you like your room cleaned now?" I asked.

"Yes, please." She smiled.

That was odd. Most visitors leered at you with a condescending air that made you feel insignificant, or they sent you away.

She watched me strip the bed.

"My husband is out buying breakfast. He should return soon."

"That's good." I didn't know what else to say.

"You know I used to clean rooms myself."

"Oh, really?" I glanced at her while spreading out a sheet. She was the first occupant I'd met who had been a chambermaid.

"Yup. I know how it is. The dirty rooms, the low pay, the tremendous back pain. No one cares, ever says thank you. Some days you feel like a slave, working for nothing." She glanced around the room. "I hope we weren't too messy."

"No, not at all." I laughed. If only other guests were as neat.

"Could I help you with that?"

I slipped on new pillowcases. "No, I'm fine."

"Makes me feel guilty," she confessed with a giggle.

"No need. This is my job." I tried to sound pleasant. Some kind of withered flower by the television caught my eye. Purple like stone.

"Do you work here every day?" she asked.

I nodded. "Weekends and a few extra nights. I'm saving up for college."

"I find that admirable."

"Thank you." Again, I didn't know what to say.

"What will you study?"

"Teaching. My father is an English teacher at my high school." I should have said *was,* only I didn't feel like getting into it.

"That's very good," she said.

Once more, I nodded.

"Yes, I love to read, too," she said, lifting up the Bible in front of her.

I finished dusting.

"You know," she continued, "reading is a whole education in itself."

Nodding a third time, I felt like a puppet on a string.

"Yes, I love to read."

"It's fun," I said, unable to think of anything profound. Again, the flower captured my attention, its lavender ribbon still bright.

"That's from my granddaughter's wedding."

"Really?"

"Yes, my Jackie got married. Right by the water. Her Marvin got two weeks leave for the honeymoon. Wasn't it nice of the Navy to give him time off from the base?"

I touched the flower. Even though it was starched like a doily, I tried to picture what it once looked like, tried to imagine its fragrance sweet like candy. "I'm sure it was a beautiful ceremony."

"It was. Marvin in his uniform, Jackie in her chiffon gown. Holding those gorgeous white lilies. Family all around. It was lovely!" She leaned toward me and winked. "A wonderful dinner, too."

I smiled.

She sipped from a glass of water, then said, "Just beautiful, like the wedding of Cana."

I excused myself to clean the bathroom.

Polishing the mirror, I thought about how Jackie's father gave her away. My father would never be able to do that. But with my track record, there probably wouldn't even be a wedding.

After I finished the bathroom, I stepped back into the room and wished the woman well.

She snapped her purse shut, struggled to stand, then wobbled toward me with her cane, the noise of jingling coins in her hand.

"Here, this is for you," she said with her hand outstretched.

"Oh, you don't have to."

"No, I'd like to."

I looked into her glistening eyes and saw youth.

"All right," I agreed.

She placed the gift into my hand.

"Thank you," I mumbled. "Thank you very much."

"You're welcome, child. It's not much, but it will help. Every little thing helps."

"You're right."

"Now what's your name?"

"Cindy O'Neill."

"Well, Cindy, you keep reading. And no matter what obstacles you face, you overcome them and be happy." Pointing to the corsage, she added, "A rose only lasts a little while before it dies."

"I will," I said, as if entranced.

Out in the hall, Toni Miles scooped a feeble handful of soap from the bowl on my cart. "I need more mints. You got some?"

I shook my head. My hand remained closed. When I finally opened it, I found four quarters, lying on my sweaty palm.

Veteran Toni walked up to me, stared down on my hand, then back at my eyes. "Well, they musta been from Brad Pitt to get you that dazed." Then she sighed heavily and walked with heavy hips back to her cart.

I smiled and stored the quarters safely in my pocket. They would stay there to remind me of my goal to save for college; for better, for worse, through thick and thin.

Jill appeared, smiling. "I'm going home."

"Condon gave you permission to leave early?"

"No. I quit."

"You can't."

"I can, and I just did." Jill removed her apron. "It was a crummy job anyway."

I grabbed a napkin from the cart and scribbled my phone number on it. Handing it to Jill, I said, "Listen, maybe your cousin wouldn't mind giving me a call sometime."

She gave me a hug. "Good for you. Actually, I'll see him at the christening. Don't worry. I'll put in a good word for you."

"Thanks."

The smile drained from her face. "Cindy, be careful. Condon might have it in for you next."

I tapped my palm against my pocket. "I can handle it."

Smiling, I pushed my cart to the next room.

NANCY MANNING's work has appeared in an eclectic mix of magazines, including *Aries, Connecticut English Journal,* and *Twilight Ending.* Her chapbook of poetry, *Amethyst Garden,* was published in October 2002. Coupled with these publishing credits, she teaches English classes at Post University, Waterbury, Connecticut.

Bolton Mountain

John Marin.
White Mountain Country.
Watercolor on paper,
20 x 27½, 1927.
Collection of Arizona
State University Art
Museum, Tempe.
Gift of Oliver B. James.
©2008 Estate
of John Marin / Artists
Rights Society (ARS),
New York.

AS THE DEPARTURE DATE LOOMED, our Long Trail backpacking trip, planned for months, started to look dicey. The weather forecast predicted two days of sun and two days of rain. Connie put it out quite firmly that she only wanted to go if the weather was good—all four days. I said, have there been four consecutive days of good weather in this entire summer?

I was desperate to go, desperate to get out of my cold, silent house, which had seemed far too empty since my old dog died. I couldn't seem to adjust to the lifelessness of the house without a dog in it, and I hadn't had enough energy the last couple of months to do much more than lie on the couch and read. I knew I needed to get up and out in the woods.

I cajoled. I begged. I bullied. I couldn't sway her. I suggested that if the weather was too nasty, we could stay in the shelter all day and meditate and write. She thought that might work. The problem was I'm not sure either one of us mentioned this "rainy day plan" to Janet, our third companion.

The first day was summer perfect. After car shuttling and driving we got on the trail mid-afternoon. We hiked a few miles uphill to Buchanan Shelter and settled in for the night. It was a sweet little place with a big open porch and a nice table where you could sit and look into the golden beech forest. We watched the sunset and made a fire. The quarter moon dropped into the hills.

During the night the rain came thundering down on the shelter's metal roof. We slept in, then drank tea on our pretty porch until 9 AM. Then Janet said, "Should we go?" "Okay," I said. Connie didn't say "no way," so we packed up and went.

The section of the trail between Buchanan and the next shelter, 4.6 miles, climbed over Bolton Mountain at 3,700 feet. It was a long ascent over a dragon's back of ever-higher peaks leading at last to the top of its head. The terse description of the day's hike in the GMC guide did not mention the slippery wet leaves and moss, the rock ledges too high to get up or down without flinging your heavily weighted body into space or sliding on your backside, or the slick tree roots that twisted out of the earth like sculpture.

It had rained hard during the night, and the trail was a trough filled with cold mud and water. I had a difficult time finding anything solid to put my boot on, and soon I sank into muddy water so deep, the water poured in over the top in a race to drown my socks. It was a cold 50-degree rain, and I was underdressed with only a thin cotton shirt under my rain jacket. We expected the day to warm up, but it didn't. After a couple of hours, my shirt was soaked and began to suck out my body heat like a reverse air conditioner.

The truth is I was so happy to be in the hills, and I didn't even mind the discomfort. I'm good at toughing out a miserable day on the trail. I chanted my mantras and sang Broadway tunes with Connie making up silly lyrics as we went along. *The hills are alive with the sound of raindrops and mud it has made for a thousand years.* Nothing all that clever, just something to take our minds off the cold and wet. It was so beautiful up there on Bolton Mountain—almost magical. The wind had torn off large clusters of orange Mountain Ash berries and tossed them on the green sphagnum moss. In one section of the trail a carpet of princess pine stretched out like an estate lawn. Streams burst down the hillsides through yellow-leaved hobblebush and blue clintonia berries. It was fall at that elevation, and the foliage was at peak. Maybe I had been longing to climb Bolton Mountain with a cold fifty-degree drizzle running down my neck.

Three times we assumed we were approaching the summit, and three times we crested a peak only to descend and climb some more. Then we crossed a ski trail, and our path took a sharp left turn and began to ascend a long steep staircase of natural stone steps with enough water rushing down them to give the impression of wading up a cascade. "There go my dry boots," Connie muttered as she pressed forward. Janet refused to believe this waterfall and trail were one. Oh, it was bad. I'm not sure how far off the idiot meter this day's stroll was, but it was definitely off—way off.

Finally the mist lifted for about two seconds, and we could see the top of Bolton Mountain looming over us to the left like a wooded Egyptian pyramid. "Oh, no" we chorused in unison, which would have been funny if our legs didn't ache, and our hands hadn't curled into red frozen claws. But a Zen master would have said to eat the cold and, really, was there any other choice?

Finally we cleared the summit and descended to Puffer Shelter at 3,200 feet. It was not the warm cozy haven we had imagined. It looked bleak. It clung to the side of the mountain like a limpet to a rock. It had a beautiful view of gray fog. Every few minutes, a gust of wind would blow some inside, right in our faces. Only the back half of the floor was dry.

We piled inside with dripping bodies and gear and did our best to keep dry. . . . The wet things had to come off. My stiff frozen hands could neither pull off my shirt nor clutch the gas knob on the stove hard enough to turn it on. Soon enough though, we were layered into warm dry things and were in our sleeping bags, drinking hot tea.

Around 4 PM it stopped raining. By 6:30 we were warm. We wrote a group haiku, the gist of which was how you have to know cold and wet before you can know warm and dry. The mist began to blow away on the breath of the wind, and we got occasional glimpses of lights twinkling on in the valley below us. There were other human beings out there in the world.

I lay in my sleeping bag after Connie and Janet had gone to sleep and thought about how fragile our safety net is, how very precarious our hot-blooded pulsing life is. I remembered clumping up the granite staircase through the rushing water and how cold I was. I remember thinking, *if you fall down now and break something, maybe you will die.* But I didn't want to die anymore. I wanted to live and to get to Puffer Shelter and warm myself. And this simple choosing of life, this re-dedication to it, was nothing more than the same choice I have to make every day; I just hadn't been able to make it for the last couple of months. And so I went to sleep grateful for not only my warm, dry sleeping bag, but also this day's bit of misery, for Bolton Mountain's tortuous trails and the cold, wet weather. There is, after all, nothing like a wet, cold slap in the face to wake you up.

LANI WRIGHT is currently teaching English at a Tsunami Relief School in southern Thailand. She has been teaching and traveling in Southeast Asia since September 2007.

VINCENT DeCAROLIS

Golden Doughnuts of the Nile

I've long forgotten
who delivered the milk,
but the man who brought pastries
in a shiny, black truck
with doors in the back
that resembled a giant butterfly
when he threw them open . . .

his uniform was also black,
as was his bow tie,
the vinyl clip-on kind because
this was nineteen fifty-six.

So I made a connection,
having seen a similar man,
at the back of a similar truck,
at the cemetery.

But the bow-tie man
is the one I remember,
and today,
because it is late November,
he comes back as he was
when the mornings were cold
and the glazing icy

on the doughnuts he stacked
in boxes so fresh and clean
it seemed to me a pharaoh
could have been laid to rest
in his cakey hearse,
his heavenly boat
with doors
that opened like the morning.

VINCENT DECAROLIS lives in Freeport, Maine, and devotes most of his time to writing poetry and fiction. His life-long scholarly interests have centered mostly around James Joyce and C.G. Jung.

COLE F. GOULET

Part of Me
Is You

All I remember is the damp smell of Old Spice,
your faded red plaids and big brown hearing aids,

your tan yet wrinkled face and the smooth fingers
that scooped me onto your lap and held me there.

I can barely recall your rough Polish accent,
the wooden TV, the gardens surrounding

the little blue house my mother grew up in.
I remember stories, though, of the long hours

you spent working with leather in your shop,
repairing clothing, wallets, and shoes,

sneaking cigarettes behind the tool shed.
The last thing I remember is not crying

when Mom told us you had passed on.
I remember not crying on the weathered porch

at Dad's new condo, too young to realize
I would never get a chance to know you at all.

So many nights I close my eyes when all is
silent, and I search for memories,

memories I've forgotten, and I wonder
which part of me is you, if you can hear me.

I wonder if it's you, up late so many nights,
stitching together poems like a torn suede jacket.

COLE GOULET, winner of the 2008 Bailey Prize for poetry, is a senior completing his English major and writing minor. He's been writing for as long as he can remember, and after rediscovering his love for poetry, Cole began taking courses with Daniel Donaghy in fall 2007. The Swedenborg Foundation thanks Professor Donaghy, assistant professor of English at Eastern Connecticut State University, for entering Cole's work in the annual Bailey Prize literary competition.

The Metzger Brothers

"COME," SAID MY MOTHER shrugging into her coat and helping me on with mine. "We will go to the Metzger (the butcher) and buy your favorite sausage for dinner."

It was September 1938, a lovely fall day. I was ten and did not need a second invitation. A visit to that shop always meant tasty little sausage pieces, which the friendly Herr Herzberg gave to all of his customers' children. Mother liked to serve fried liver with onions, mashed potatoes, and sauerkraut, cooked with grated apple, onion, caraway and celery seeds, but tonight she would make my most favorite dish in the world: a casserole with mashed potatoes on the bottom, a layer of sausage cut into chunks, a layer of sauerkraut, and topped with mashed potatoes sprinkled with butter and crumbs.

Down the street we went, softly chatting and laughing together, quietly of course, because we didn't want to call attention to ourselves. One was so conscious of being Jewish in those days, and we never knew who might hurl an insult at us. We turned into the street where the shop was located, and Mother gasped. The large front window was broken, and a large Star of David was painted on the sidewalk. Mom held on to me tightly, squared her shoulders, and entered the store. Herr Herzberg, stout and bald with glasses, was trying to tape the broken glass together while Mrs. Herzberg, tall with deep worry lines on her forehead, swept the floor. We both smiled sadly at them.

"Ah, Frau Stern," he said, as he shook Mother's hand. "You are my first customer today. That deserves a special treat." He walked behind his counter and cut off a good-sized piece of liver sausage and handed it to me while Mother and Mrs. Herzberg talked in low tones. I overheard her telling Mutti, "I am glad that my in-laws are dead. They worked so hard to establish the business, and I know they would have been terribly shocked with this destruction. And did you see what they did outside? The boys are away at the university, but that may not last. I am really worried about Elsa who is fifteen and so pretty. I just don't know what to do!"

Mom bought more than just sausage. Perhaps she sensed that this store would not stay open for long. I helped her carry two heavy bags home. She was quiet and pensive. The prospect of a delicious dinner did not seem as exciting anymore. I never saw the butcher again. On November 8 strict laws were passed regulating Jewish lives. Within two days my parents sent me, along with my cousin Werner, to Amsterdam in 1938 to live with my father's sister, Aunt Frieda. They hoped that we would be safe there for the time being. A few months later our parents were able to come to Holland where we all waited until our immigration permits for the U.S. were issued in 1940.

FORWARD TO APRIL 1992. My husband, Edward, my sister Lotte with husband Irvin, cousins Annelies and Suzy and husbands were to meet in Aachen for our Survivors' Reunion. Most of the German cities had held those events for their former Jewish citizens, and Aachen was one of the last to issue the invitation.

Edward and I flew from Denver to Chicago and had a four-hour layover for Lufthansa to take us to Frankfurt. As we were sitting, we looked around wondering who also might be going to Aachen or who looked familiar to me. We noticed a couple several rows away who dressed just as my parents used to. The man was dressed in a suit, starched shirt, and tie, while the woman wore a suit, a blouse with ruffles at the neck, and high heels.

"Honey," I turned to my husband, "I am sure they are going to Aachen."

We took the travel papers we had received in the mail and passed them back and forth to each other. We were successful! The couple noticed us, spoke to one another, and the gentleman came over.

"Are you going to Aachen?" he asked.

"Yes, are you also?"

"Yes, what is your name please?"

"Liesel Shineberg, this is my husband, Edward, and my maiden name was Stern."

"Max Stern?"

I had goose pimples on my arms. "Yes, did you know my father?"

He looked at his wife, "I told you she looked just like her mother."

I was speechless. My birth mother died when I was nine months old. I never knew her and here, out of the blue, was someone who recognized my resemblance to my mother fifty years later.

I asked him, "What is your name?"

"Klaus Hellman. Does that mean anything to you? I am a nephew of Herr Professor Levy."

I did remember that name. He was a close friend of my father's. I joined the Hellmans, and they told me all they remembered about my birth mother. I knew then that this was going to be a hell of a trip!

The only international airport was in Frankfurt, and everyone was bussed to Aachen. It was a long trip and, once in our room at the hotel, Edward took a nap. I was too excited and went downstairs to wait for other busses to arrive with my California family.

A bus stopped. A man, shorter than I with thick glasses, who had been standing next to me, stepped forward, watching people disembark. We were both disappointed. We stepped back enjoying the sight of people who had not seen one another in years greeting, laughing, and crying together. My neighbor looked at me.

"My brother," he explained in broken English. "Israel," he said pointing to himself. I used my rusty German to tell him I was waiting for my sister and cousins. We did not have time to exchange names as another bus pulled up. A tall and heavily built man stepped off. My neighbor slowly walked toward him.

"Oh God, it *is* you!" he cried, holding out his arms.

"Werner, thank God!"

The two embraced, laughing and crying, hugging and holding. A woman stood next to them wiping tears from her eyes. Suddenly the smaller man saw her.

"Oh, Elsa," he said. "It's too long! You look just like our mother."

The next bus held my family. Although we see each other at least once a year, being together in our old hometown was very special. We went to our rooms, expecting to meet later to sign in, have a glass of wine, and eat dinner.

At 5 o'clock, we received name badges, often with our maiden names, and with our age, and city and country of current residency. We would wear those name tags during our stay not only for fellow returnees to identify us, but also to let the local populace know who we were. A lady came close to me, looked at my badge and said, "Liesel, do you remember me? I used to be Britta Lyon."

"Britta!!! How are you? Where are you now and is your little mother still with us?"

"You remember my Mom?"

"Oh yes, she was the smallest and daintiest person I had ever seen. I never forgot her. She made great cookies." Tears welled in her eyes.

"My mother died four months ago. She had looked forward to this trip, but she had heart problems. She passed away in her sleep. I still miss her." After a quick hug, we were led to the dining room. Looking around the table, I saw my companion who'd waited with me for the bus. He signaled for Edward and me to sit close to them, and we started to compare names and former occupations. The taller brother, Karl, knew just enough English that he and Ed could converse using lots of body language. This is the story he told.

Werner, eighteen, and Karl, twenty years old, were away at a university boarding school when Mr. Herzberg, their father, called them home. Karl was tall with brown hair and built like a natural athlete and soccer player. Werner was smaller and slight with black, curly hair and thick glasses. They stood out because of their Jewish appearance.

"You two will have to hide because we hear that all the Jews in Aachen will soon be deported to the East. I'm going to ask Herr Schmitz, the farmer who supplies me with our beef, if you can both work for him and stay out of sight."

"What about Elsa, you, and Mom?" asked Werner.

"Mutti and I will stay together, and I will ask the priest at the church if he knows of a place for Elsa."

Herr Schmitz agreed to take the boys back to the country, and what a sad farewell it was. Elsa found a temporary place with a Catholic family until something permanent could be arranged.

Karl and Werner found themselves in a strange environment. Neither knew a thing about farming or animals. Herr Schmitz took them to the barn where his old horse was stabled. "My horse is getting a bit long in the tooth and won't be able to pull the plow much longer. So, you two will be my horses. You will pull the machinery and whatever else needs to be done. I will feed you well to keep you strong, but you must live in the barn when work is over. You will keep your mouths shut and stay out of sight as much as possible. Understand?"

And so it went for four years! They were hitched to the plow, planted, carried water into the fields, cut hay, pulled the wagons to feed the animals, and helped with slaughter. During the cold winter, they spent their time mending machinery, sewing sacks for hay carried into the fields for cows, and repaired their clothing to keep warm.

It was during the first winter that Mr. Schmitz came into the barn. "I am sorry to have to tell you that your parents were picked up last week and shipped to Poland."

"What about Elsa?" asked Karl.

"I don't know, and I'm not going to ask either."

The two young men, fairly safe themselves, were beside themselves with worry. The Jews knew about the camps in the east, but as far as they knew then, the extermination camps were only a rumor. They understood, however, that rumors are often based on facts, so they clung together, giving each other courage when one or the other faltered. They dreamed of being reunited with their family and released from the bondage in which they found themselves.

In 1944, during spring and summer, they saw and heard planes heading eastward. Mr. Schmitz looked glum and worried. Werner developed a respiratory infection and grew weaker. Karl worked twice as hard to cover for him. They heard bombs falling and cannon fire from the west. More planes flew even closer in the fall. In winter food became scarce. It was just after Christmas when the Allied Forces crossed the river Wurm into Aachen. Herr Schmitz left the area with his family to escape the Allies. Tanks and infantry crossed the fields and found Werner and Karl hiding in the barn.

"Who are you? What are you doing here?" asked one of the soldiers in German.

"We are Jews who were hiding on this farm. We are from Aachen."

"Jews? I don't believe you."

"Yes, really we are Jews!" Karl started to drop his pants to prove that he was circumcised.

"OK, OK, we believe you. But your brother looks bad."

As if to answer, Werner coughed and coughed and spat blood.

"Let's take the boy to the infirmary," said the soldier. "You," pointing to Karl, "come with us. You know the area and can be useful."

"I can't leave my brother. He's all that's left from my family."

"He'll be taken care of, and you can come back for him when he is well."

So Karl went with the advance troops, using his native language where needed, and helped to scout out the Aachener woods and surroundings. Weeks dragged into months before he could look for Werner. His brother had been sent to England for hospitalization with other wounded, and Karl was unable to locate him. Karl was sent to a relocation camp and ended up in Canada. Through the Red Cross he was able to find Elsa, who had survived Bergen-Belsen, and he secured a visa for her. The two tried through the years to find their younger brother, Werner. Before obtaining Canadian citizenship, Karl and Elsa changed their name to Metzger in honor of their family and profession. Karl married, had several children, and established his own grocery store in Toronto, featuring the best meat in town.

Werner had emigrated to Israel and tried through all channels to learn if his brother and sister had survived. The American Red Cross had no lists of survivors outside the U.S. Werner learned Hebrew, returned to school, obtained a business degree in Haifa, and found a job as a manager of a grocery chain. He married a sabra, a native born Israeli, and had two girls. To honor his departed family, he changed his name to Metzger.

For the 1992 Aachen reunion of survivors, lists of returnee names with current addresses and phone numbers were sent out. We all searched them in hopes of finding familiar names. Werner found his name and right above, alphabetically, saw the name Karl Metzger. His heart lurched—could it be? Was it possible? He picked up the phone, which rang and rang. While it was afternoon in Israel, it was the middle of the night in Canada. Finally a woman's voice answered.

Werner spoke in German, "This is Werner Herzberg Metzger. May I speak with Karl?"

"Herzberg? Wait, wait, I call Karl!" Werner heard the woman screaming to her husband. "Herzberg, on the phone, he said Herzberg. Quick!"

A man's voice said, "Who is this?"

"Karl, speak German. This is Werner. Is this really you?"

Karl fell back into his chair. "Werner, you are still alive?"

"I must be! I am speaking to you from Israel. I looked for you for so long. I did not dream that you would be in Canada!"

"Oh my God. I must call Elsa first thing in the morning."

"Elsa is with you?"

"Yes, married and a grandmother. We have so much to talk about. I prayed so hard that we might find you someday!"

Elsa was a warm, plump, funny, and pleasant lady, who proudly wore short-sleeved garments whenever possible. Often, when asked about the numbers tattooed on her arm by the Nazis, she would reply that her memory often failed her. "This is my phone number," she smiled, "I will never get lost as long as I can read that." Black humor but it served her well.

I shared my memory of shopping with my mother at their store so long ago. I told them of their father's generosity whenever I visited. His sausage was the best. His wife often said how he loved to make children smile when he gave them little treats.

So here we were, fifty years later, in our old world—a joyous occasion but a sad one. Lotte and I found our biological mother's grave and were finally able to utter the *Yis Gadal*, the prayer for the dead, for her soul. The Metzgers—they never stopped talking!

Born in Aachen, Germany, in 1928, LIESEL SHINEBERG, attended school there until Jewish children were no longer allowed public education. While living in Holland with her aunt (1938–1940), she was a schoolmate of Anne Frank. It was not until Germany invited former refugees to survivor reunions that she realized the importance of sharing these early experiences. She now speaks regularly in schools, churches, and other gatherings, and is hard at work on her memoirs. One of her stories is in the archive of the Holocaust Museum in Washington, D.C. Liesel lives with her husband in Rock Springs, Wyoming, where she attends classes at Western Wyoming College. The Swedenborg Foundation thanks Professor Richard Kempa for entering her story in the 2008 Bailey Prize competition.

Build Your Research Library!
Chrysalis Reader Bargains!

Save on back issues of the Chrysalis Reader with this special offer *($10 per package)*.

Time & Essence p a c k a g e

Reader volume and title:

Volume 5   Seeing through Symbols: *Insights into Spirit*
Volume 7   Rocking the Ages: *The Pulse and Continuity of Change*
Volume 13   Passages: *Timeless Voyages of Spirit*

Community & Chaos p a c k a g e

Reader volume and title:

Volume 1   Gold from Aspirin: *Spiritual Views on Chaos and Order*
Volume 2   Twelve Gates to the City: *Spiritual Views on the Journey*
Volume 12   Embracing Relationships

Bliss & Laughter p a c k a g e

Reader volume and title:

Volume 3   The Power of Play: *New Visions in Creativity*
Volume 4   Going for It!: *Thirty-six Views on the Good Life*

Profound Living p a c k a g e

Reader volume and title:

Volume 9   Chances Are: *Providence? Serendipity? or Fate?*
Volume 14   Imagine That!: *Breaking Through to Other Worlds*

Spiritual Growth p a c k a g e

Reader volume and title:

Volume 8   Live & Learn: *Perspectives on the Questing Spirit*
Volume 10   Eternal Wellness: *The Importance of Healing,*
                    Connecting, Community, and the Inner Journey

Challenging Choices p a c k a g e

Reader volume and title:

Volume 6   Decisions! Decisions!: *The Dynamics of Choice*
Volume 11   Letting Go: *Living Without a Net*

To order, please contact:

Swedenborg Foundation Publishers • *Illuminating the spiritual life*
1-800-366-3222, ext. 10 • customerservice@swedenborg.com • www.swedenborg.com